Cary Tennis

That
Special Time
of Year

CARY TENNIS BOOKS, LLC
San Francisco

The columns first appeared on Salon.com

FIRST EDITION

Tennis, Cary.
That Special Time of Year / by Cary Tennis.

ISBN-13: 978-0-9793270-2-5
1. Self Help—Advice. 2. Essays—Advice.

Printed in the United States of America

10 9 8 7 6 5 4 3 2 1

Book design by Norma Tennis
Cary Tennis illustration by Zach Trenholm

Contents

Introduction

Dear Reader,

EVERY TIME ANY writer anywhere sits down to write, he or she has a problem. On the one hand there is a message to convey. In this case: Here is a wonderful collection of holiday-themed columns. I hope you enjoy them. At the same time, every meeting between reader and writer is an opportunity to alter the course of someone's life, and every moment is sacred and irreplaceable, and thus one might as well act with boldness and courage. So if you are stuck or in trouble or conflicted about your course in life, let me remind you that you have the power to make the choice that is right for your conscience and your circumstance, in spite of your momentary fears. For instance, if you are trying to decide whether to visit your family for the holidays even though you are concerned about money, in the words of the first column in this collection, I might suggest that you go because it is an act of faith to do what you feel you ought to do and trust that things will work out.

My guiding principle is that each encounter between writer and reader is not just an occasion when needed information passes from one to the other, but a shared moment when we both stand on a precipice and contemplate together the vastness before us.

So I wish to say that I'm proud of this collection of columns and I hope you enjoy them and I hope you order some books to give to your friends, and I also wish to say that if you have a sick relative you have not spoken to in quite some time but think of occasionally and wonder how she's doing, why not put this book down right now and give her a call because no one is around forever and life passes quickly. One tries to convey some needed information, and, at the same time, to awaken the reader to the holiness of every second, to the possibilities of every moment to get up from our desks or our chairs and out into the world to feel the sunshine as if for the first time, knowing always that any day may be our last day, and any person we see we may be seeing for the last time.

And that is how I get from A to B on this particular sunny Sunday morning in San Francisco—by saying what has to be said and also to hint at what is in some sense unsayable.

I hope you enjoy these holiday-themed columns. Now go outside and look at the sky and say your name to yourself. Remember who you are, and who you are meant to be.

Cary Tennis
San Francisco

That
Special Time
of Year

Should we go home for Christmas—even if we can't afford it?

We lost our house in Katrina. The family is scattered but gathering. Should we go?

Dear Cary,

SO CHRISTMAS, THE so-called happiest time of the year, fast approaches, and my little family is in a tough situation. Over the last year or so, my girlfriend and I have had many stressful, good and bad, life-changing events—we lost our home in New Orleans due to Katrina, had our first child, and eventually, after a few stops along the way, relocated to New York City. We're a pretty tough crew, and things are going well enough generally, but our Christmas plans are now a mangled mess and I am not sure how to handle it. We planned, months ago, to join my side of the family for Christmas for five days in the middle of the country. My family is scattered to the wind, so this is a big deal for everyone. The tickets are purchased, my folks, siblings, and other relatives are traveling long distances for the holiday, and our little girl is certainly a major reason everyone is getting together this year. But now my girlfriend believes it is a bad idea for us to go for financial reasons and wants us to cancel.

On a certain level, she's right. She has just started waiting tables after staying at home with the baby for year, and we don't have much money right now, so the extra bit helps. This visit would mean she would likely

1

lose her job, so she'd have to find another one immediately upon return. My income covers most of our expenses, which are quite numerous here in New York, but we'll soon need to start paying a babysitter or daycare, and we should probably start paying off some of our credit card debt. We could have Christmas with her family, who live nearby and we see often, and she could work extra holiday shifts.

On the other hand, we would survive if we were to keep our plans. She will begin a career track in February that will soon net her a much more sustainable wage than waiting tables, and combined with my full-time employment, we'll be on solid ground later this year. There are a million waiting gigs around here, so she could start working almost immediately post-Christmas. We're not broke, rent will get paid, and Christmas is an important holiday to us. I feel like we have an obligation to our family, as we were somewhat central in the planning of this, and the other parts of my family may have planned differently (like flying here or waiting until later to get together). I just feel like this is a no-win situation, and our communication around this sucks—we are both frustrated with each other and can't find any common ground. I feel like if we don't go, we've deprived our child from being with my seldom-seen relatives at an important juncture in her life. My girlfriend feels like if we do go, I am not accepting financial reality and pushing her to do something that means losing her job and us losing money. So I guess I have a few questions wrapped up in this dilemma. Should I keep pushing for us to go? Should I simply go by myself? Should I take the baby along and work through an unplanned weaning process over a holiday? Should I accept this makes some financial sense and cancel on my family? You have any other ideas for us to avoid a miserable holiday? Thanks so much.

Stuck in Indecision

Dear Stuck,

GO. GO BECAUSE the tickets are bought. Go because everybody wants to see the little girl. You will be taken care of. Go. Go because no, you shouldn't go. Go because no, it may not be so smart. Go. Go because your family is getting together. Go because you can't choose the year your family gets together. Go.

Go because the holidays are not about sensible. Go because you belong there. Go because your family needs you and you need your family and this is how you're supposed to do it. Go because this is what a family is: A family is a group that just goes. It doesn't make the sensible decisions all the time. Go because people draw strength from each other. Go because it's good to do the right thing when it's difficult. Go because you're setting a good example.

Go because it is an act of faith to do what you feel you ought to do and trust that things will work out. Go because you don't want to show weakness and fear. Go because you want to act as if things are going to work out. Go because I just bought a dining room set and a pool table and I don't want to be the only one stupid enough to get carried away with the holidays and just do what he probably can't afford and shouldn't do but what brings some joy into the world. Go because my truck needs some body work. Go because my uncle is dying. Go because I'm going to miss my family when they're gone and so are you. Go because Katrina happened and you never know. Go because waitress jobs are a dime a dozen. Go because your family needs to see that you are OK.

Go because this is the land of freedom and open spaces and just going for it. Go because you want to. Go because string theory says there are probably 11 dimensions, and in at least one of those dimensions you would be going anyway. Go because if you don't go the terrorists win. Go because I'm getting increasingly desperate. Go because I'm really grasping at straws now. Go because if you don't go my writing is going to get worse and worse. Go because self-referentiality weakens the soul and is bad for the digestion. Go. Just go. Apologize to your wife. Say it's my fault. Blame it on me. Just go.

I'm already dreading
Christmas with my family

We'll sit around with nothing to say, eating takeout food.

Dear Cary,

I KNOW THIS is pretty early, but I'm already freaking out about hanging out with my family during Christmas. My family consists of my mother, my father, my brother and me, the daughter/sister. My brother isn't married, but I am; I have a husband and two kids. My husband and the kids get along fine with my family; actually, my parents love my husband to pieces. The problem is with me.

Whenever I get together with my parents, which is only once a year or so, I get the feeling that they don't really want to be with me. I mean, we drive six hours, they fly for four hours and my brother flies for four hours (don't ask why we are all traveling...that is another long story) and then we spend the weekend together by doing a lot of nothing. My parents go to sleep at 7 or 8 p.m. and get up at 5 a.m., and by the time I get up at 7:30 a.m. or so, they have already left to go to doctors appointments, to fix the roof on a rental house, to go to the DMV. They don't show up until noon or so. My brother stays in bed until 2 p.m. and parties with his friends until late. Our "quality time" together consists of eating from the same takeout places over and over again.

Now that I have toddlers, there is something to entertain us, but without the kids, there is nothing to say to each other. My parents are very private people; if you asked me what their biggest worry was,

I would have no idea. When I ask about their work, I just get vague answers and sort of sarcastic replies. I know this is just par for the course because I have the same problem getting all defensive about choices I made and things that I do; when they ask me questions, I hedge as well. I've made some career choices that bother them and they let me know that they don't like it, so I shut up about the details. My mother also recently told me that she would like to divorce my dad because he's kind of a control freak and generally a rude man, except that she takes her wedding vows seriously and that she's used to him and, heck, what else would she do? This was a shock to me (even though I think I could never live with my dad) as I thought that their marriage was fine, even stellar.

I just have this feeling that we are at an impasse, that all of us want to be closer but we don't know how to be. Right now, I feel that hanging out with my parents is an obligation rather than something I enjoy. Is it to be that way always? If it is, I just want to know that and that I shouldn't expect any more closeness from my family and I should look elsewhere. I've been reading a lot of Zen stuff recently and I've been trying to let go of my "attachment" to having a close family and have no expectations of ever having one, but I have to say, sometimes I read stories of people's relationships with their parents changing on their deathbeds and their wishing it had happened earlier. My relationship with my parents isn't terrible—it's just not very much fun. What should I do?

Out of Sorts

Dear Out of Sorts,

YOU CAN CHANGE your eye color. You can change your sex. You can change the temperature of the planet. But you can't change your family.

What you can do is introduce small variations in the activities you engage in while visiting with your family. These activities may have the effect of changing how you feel while you're around them. One of the things you might try is just to be a positive, supportive witness.

See if there are ways you can be helpful, without getting in the way. You might offer to drive your parents around on their early-morning errands, or to accompany them in their car to expedite the parking and waiting as they go in and out of places. As you accompany them, perhaps riding in the back seat, observe them. Look at them closely. Think about who they are. Consider them as individuals. Let your mind wander. Be Zen-like about it.

There will probably be a lot of stupid and boring stuff coming out of their mouths. Try not to get any on you. Let it pass. Be a supportive witness to their experience. Hold a place in line at the DMV. Hand your mother a magazine. Hold her purse while she looks for her other glasses. Be unobtrusively helpful, and observe. Observe your mother and observe yourself. What are you doing as you stand there, holding her purse for her? Are you resenting her for being so befuddled? Are you mad at her for telling you she'd like to divorce your dad but probably never will? Does it give you a sinking feeling? A feeling of rage? Are you wishing you were somewhere else, anywhere other than here? Where is it exactly that you would like to be? Make a mental note to go there, later, after Christmas. Then get back to what you are doing, holding your mother's purse, glancing at the magazines in the waiting room.

The idea is to get your bearings. Get comfortable being around your parents. Lower your expectations until they touch reality.

You may wish to make some breakthrough by talking about the things that are on your mind—why doesn't the family come together like a family, dammit?! But you must be careful. A family is a delicate thing, wrathful and sensitive to disturbance. If there are certain things that you feel need to be discussed, it might be best to approach them not as emotional or spiritual questions, but as tasks that need performing. It sounds like your parents are practical people who value getting things done in a timely manner. So if, for instance, there are questions of health, or life and death, that you feel your parents and your brother avoid talking about, you might approach them by attempting to square away financial concerns, powers of attorney, investments, the will.

For certain kinds of people, a troubling spiritual question is best addressed in its physical embodiment. For such people, the proper

6

disposition of such an embodiment can, in itself, constitute a spiritual or emotional experience. I know that sounds rather arid to those of us who breathe deeply of the bracing air in the world of ideas, but in my experience it is often the case.

You must go slowly, respecting the depth and complexity of the family as an organism. To be realistic, in this first year of trying to make it better, you might only accomplish small variations in your own activities.

Because of your dissatisfaction with how the family performs, which you probably have not successfully hidden (we can hide little from our family), other family members may already fear that you are going to try to "bring the family together." They may not want to be brought together. In fact, such enforced togetherness can be so excruciating for its victims that they find some pretext never to return.

Anything that smacks of trying to bring the family together may have the undesired effect of tearing it apart. It is, as I said, a fragile thing.

So I suggest you make such changes as you can in your own activities, quietly, meditatively, without attachment to result. Try to be a reliable, supportive witness to those around you. Hope for gradual improvement.

My mother sends me
useless junk for Christmas

She shops all year for "bargains" and then boxes up
all this weird, inappropriate merchandise.

Dear Cary,

HELP!

Every year my mother sends us holiday gifts, even though she has little to no extra money. She buys things all year round "on sale" and stores useless items in a closet in her house. During the holidays, she packs up a bunch of stuff, puts it in a box, and sends it to me and my sister. There is no thought put into the gifts, and I'm concerned she's a compulsive spender. I've told her as much—the year she bought me a snowman made out of coconuts and a pair of green velvet jeans four times my size.

I told her I'm concerned about her spending habits and that she's not saving any money for retirement. She insists she is going to come live with us when she retires. I told her flat out that she needs to save for her future and not count on living with us. Our relationship has been and continues to be tedious at best.

She had a very ugly divorce from my father, and when he died, she berated him constantly and still speaks negatively about him. I feel she needs help and should work out her issues—and in the meantime stop sending us thoughtless, wasteful gifts for the holidays!

How do I tell her to not keep wasting her money on us? I've told her to give to charity, to save her money, and to stop sending us gifts, period. She doesn't listen. What's the etiquette for over 10 years of worthless gifts? Every year my sister and I pack up the stuff she gives us and donate it to charity. I would really prefer my mother to keep her money rather than give us a tax write-off!

Confused Recipient

Dear Confused,

TELLING YOUR MOTHER not to send gifts is probably futile. In families that are separated geographically, sending gifts every year is a way of connecting. The gifts themselves are not the point. The point is the connection. This connection may seem rather abstract and meaningless to you. But it has some value to your mother.

As far as the kinds of gifts she's buying for you, well, she's obviously not making the best choices. Perhaps she needs better information. Why not give her a list of things that you could actually use—complete with brand names, sizes, model numbers, etc.

But it's really not about the gifts. It's about the behavior. Think of the pleasure she gets out of doing this. It's her way of connecting to you.

Your mom may not have much going on in her life. But when she goes to the store, probably alone, if she is buying things for you, then you are there with her, in a way—you are in her thoughts. As she looks for bargains, she is thinking about you. Perhaps she is reliving happy times when you and your sister were kids. By shopping for you, she continues to do the thing she found meaning in—to nourish you, take care of you. Shopping also gets her out with other people. There she is, rubbing elbows with all the others, jostling for bargains. She says to the clerk, "This is for my daughter."

It may be about the objects to some degree, but if it was just the objects, she'd do all her shopping from catalogs and online.

So if you could find a way to work with the very human impulses that are behind this behavior of hers, perhaps you could make some progress in dealing with the issues it raises. What I mean is, people do things for reasons. Although it may be a pain in the ass, it isn't senseless at all.

You link her buying of gifts with your sense that she doesn't handle her money well. These two things may well be connected. It's probably also true that your disapproval of her habits stems from the same source as her buying you gifts: familial love and a desire to help, to protect. So, proceeding on that premise: If you think your mother needs some financial planning help, then do something about it now. Don't wait 15 or 20 years to discover that she has no resources. Telling her to get her stuff together is not sufficient. That doesn't count as "doing something about it." That's just symbolic—in the same way that her buying gifts for you is just symbolic. You have to do something concrete—visit her and spend a few days going over her finances. If you can't make sense of it, hire an accountant or a financial planner. You may find that she's in better shape than you thought. Or she may be in worse shape. The important thing is to know, and then plan.

My 13=year=old still believes in Santa Claus

Should I tell her the truth—to save her from the derision of her friends, if nothing else?

Hi Cary,

I WILL BE the first to admit that this may seem like a lame problem in the full scheme of things, but I would love for you to weigh in on this. My nearly 13-year-old stepdaughter believes in Santa Claus. Completely.

To give some background, her father was widowed when she was an infant, so we are her only living parents. I also have two small children from my first marriage who are still very much in the Santa target demographic. So you might assume she's going along with the game for the younger kids, but it's truly not the case.

Last Christmas, our first as a family, I was stunned when she asked me how Santa would know to find her at her new address. And just yesterday she admitted to wondering how Santa could truly go down everyone's chimney at midnight. ("That would be impossible, even for Santa.")

Her comments and questions have all come at times when the other children are not around. She's not pretending.

This is an incredibly bright child—honor roll, advanced classes, very much a freethinker, with an amazing social consciousness. She's not stunted in her emotional development. Tooth fairy, Easter Bunny—she gave those up years ago. But Santa's legitimacy isn't even on her radar.

So here's the question my husband and I are pondering: Do we spill the beans?

I have very vivid memories from fourth grade when an insensitive teacher made a comment about Santa truly being our parents. My classmates and I were stunned when the one little girl in the class who was apparently still in the dark put her head on her desk and burst into tears. The rest of us had already known for some time. That was the early 1980s. And kids today are supposedly so much more advanced.

My husband is concerned she is going to embarrass herself around her peers. And he has a point—especially at this age where she's so overwhelmingly self-conscious about fitting in and being part of a group.

But at the same time, a part of me thinks it's kind of charming. I mean, she's had to grow up faster than her peers in some ways, having no mother around for so much of her life. Why shouldn't she be able to keep some aspects of childhood around a little longer?

Aside from preventing social embarrassment, the only other advantage I see to telling her the truth is that it would make it a little easier for her to understand why she won't receive some of the excessive gifts her peers will find under the tree on Christmas morning (iPods, computers, video game systems). I do remember from my own experience that it was quite a relief to discover that my more modest Christmas gifts weren't an indication that Santa didn't like me as much as the other kids.

I wish we could afford to do more for all three of our wonderful kids, but our oldest, because teenagers' "toys" are considerably more pricey, is the only one who is really noticing the discrepancy. Maybe it's guilt that's truly fueling this question?

I know in the full scheme of things this seems rather small and insignificant, but I would be very interested to get your opinion on this.

Wondering Mom

Dear Wondering Mom,

INSOFAR AS POSSIBLE we tell our kids the truth. But there is of course much leeway in what truths are told and how.

I think you tell her what can best be called the poetic truth. It's possible that your stepdaughter possesses a poetic soul, and that what she gets from her belief is the pleasure of beauty and magic. So it may not be terribly important to her whether it is literally true or not—what is important is that you be sensitive to what it means to her. The story of Santa is art; it is so captivating and beautiful that she may simply want to enjoy the music of it, the captivating happiness of it. That enjoyment could be shattered if too rudely explicated, but it need not be shattered at all, even as she awakens to the impossibility of Santa's most vaunted feats.

"Nobody can conceive or imagine all the wonders there are unseen and unseeable in the world," wrote Francis P. Church in his famous 1897 New York Sun editorial, "Yes, Virginia, There Is a Santa Claus."

He said pretty much what I would have said, only better.

For doubting, secular people, Christmas can still be an innocent time, a time of taking pleasure in innocent beauty. When I was a child Christmas was the only time of the year when society seemed to recognize that there is beauty and joy in the world and it can be shared and there is a time to sit together by the fire and play music and sing songs and give each other gifts. What a wonderful time.

What you want to communicate to your stepdaughter is this: the willingness to both know and believe.

I would ask her what she believes. I would respect her beliefs.

And then I think I would warn her. I would warn her—as if she did not already know—that other children can be extremely cruel, and that while it is perfectly acceptable to believe things others do not believe, it is sometimes wise to keep one's most cherished beliefs to oneself. People can trample one's beliefs. They can destroy them with a careless word or gesture. So it is sometimes best to hold one's beliefs close, to protect them from the corrosive derision of insensitive others who would trample on our dreams.

I would warn her, too, about the way people keep score with presents, and remind her that there are, in this realm too, a thousand different ways of keeping score. If she is bright, she can keep score with grades and achievement, and if she is inward-looking, she can keep score on how true she is to herself.

So encourage her to have dreams, to cultivate dreams, and to protect her dreams and her beliefs.

There are many truths. There are musical truths and sculptural truths and performance truths; there are baseball scores and mathematical theorems; there are poetic truths and observable truths and observable truths that are not true—for instance, the observable truth that the sun revolves around the Earth is an illusion. It depends on where you're standing.

And there are many things that we believe which are as yet unprovable. We believe that pi, for instance, does not repeat its digits. Having calculated it out to 200 billion digits in which as yet no pattern has been found can we yet be certain that no pattern ever will be found? What about at 200 billion billion digits? That's a lot of digits. Even 100,000 digits is a lot of digits.

So I would stand with Francis Church. Mysteries and miracles abound in the visible and invisible world. Santa is among them.

Hating the holidays

All I want for Christmas is a kind, intelligent man.
I'm starting to doubt it will ever happen.

Dear Cary,

THE HOLIDAYS ARE here, and I need to unload!

I spent Thanksgiving Day in the hospital with my ailing grandmother, and tried to console my depressed grandfather, who is going broke because of her health and only has me to depend on—I live three hours away. This Christmas marks the 15th anniversary of my mother's death. New Year's marks the 10th anniversary of a brother's death. My younger, hipster sister and her boyfriend arrive in two days, to spend three looooong weeks with me (not my idea). Don't get me started on my pothead brother whose bar band is going to "make it big once they move to L.A. ..."

This weekend my dryer broke, my car is going in for a $400 tuneup tomorrow, and I desperately need new tires to get through the Minnesota snowy-icy-salty mess we call winter. I haven't purchased a single Christmas gift yet.

I turn 30 in five months and am very single. (Being single and 30 in the Midwest is equal to having "Loser" tattooed to your forehead.) I haven't had sex in four years. I feel completely unattractive, undesirable and destined to spinsterhood. My sister tells me "you don't need a boyfriend"—this is the sister who is so codependent when she's away from her boy for more than three days she goes anorexic. Yeah, I don't need a boyfriend, but a companion to keep me sane and loved over the holidays would be fabulous.

I've considered calling my doctor for a prescription for Holiday Zoloft, but then realized it would take a few weeks to kick in and the torture of the holidays would probably be over by then. I've been exercising regularly, but those endorphins don't seem to be doing the job.

I have no desire to step foot in a shopping mall, or spend time with my family. Christmas day will consist of 8 minutes at the dinner table, me and my siblings, with dad running off to the casino to play blackjack after beating last year's dinner time of 10 minutes. I have friends I'd rather spend time with, but as the oldest sib, I can't abandon my family—the guilt is too much.

When I look at the bigger picture, I do sound whiny. I have my health, I'm good at being self-employed, there's a good chance that Bush won't be reelected next year. But it's really hard to see everyone else going to big family gatherings with their significant others...I'm feeling shortchanged.

All I want for Christmas is a kind, intelligent man. And I know it's not going to happen this year, and I'm starting to doubt it will ever happen. So how long do I have to endure the obligations of family before I can run off and spend mid-November to mid-January far, far away? Do you think I'll ever be able to enjoy the holidays? After all the ucky stuff I've been through shouldn't there be some karmic turn of events? Or do I count my blessings and accept that this is the way it's always going to be?

Hating the Holidays

Dear Hating the Holidays,

I KNOW ABOUT the holiday season and how it crashes down on you. I have struggled up out of the snow and trudged into town where all the shiny things are, where the people don't know the streets because they never come downtown except in December, where giant red sweaters with cute embroidered animals lunge at you from blind corners, where children paw your bags, where traffic resembles something you might find on planet Jupiter. I know, I know, I know.

Still, two things strike me. First, you are conspicuously absent from your own story. Second, it is not really a story but a collection of situations. They are only situations because if they were stories they would be about you and what you are trying to accomplish. Instead, there is nothing here of you and how you have tried to live through the deaths and the craziness. Perhaps that is the root of your desperation, the sense your letter gives not just of weariness and misfortune but of panic: that you have disappeared from your own story.

What were you about to do just when your mother died? Where were you headed? Did you start cooking for the younger ones then, and for your father too? Is that what you have been doing since then, caring for the rest of them? Did you even have any time to grieve after your mother died? Maybe you're still grieving, except it sounds like anger. Maybe that's what happens when we shove aside the grieving for years: It turns to a kind of impatient, panicked anger.

So go back to the time when your mother died, and play the videotape again slowly. Try to find your own face in the picture, and understand the expression on it: Are you startled, sad, amazed, frightened?

There are many reasons to resurrect this story, not just to save your soul. If you find a kind, intelligent man, for instance, he is going to want to know your story—because that is what kind, intelligent men want, aside from world peace and a better book lamp.

As you are aware, given any set of facts we can make a variety of stories. Given your set of facts, for instance, one person might say that she had had the privilege of being with her grandmother over the holidays, during what may be her ailing grandmother's last days, in a way that she perhaps wasn't able to be around when her mother was dying, or at least not as an adult, aware of the immense finality. She might say how lucky she is that her grandmother lives only three hours away, and how glad she is that her grandmother's medical care is still being taken care of by her grandfather, who though depressed can still afford to take care of his wife, although it is a bit of a financial strain. She might mention how glad she is that they are both still alive, and how grateful she is to them for being there for her after her mother died.

You get the picture. Some would call it the glass half-full/half-empty thing. But the question is, are you thirsty?

The question is, What have you been looking for? And what happened?

Maybe what you've been looking for all your life is just 10 minutes to yourself, without duty, without sadness, without tragedy and loss, without guilt. And you almost had it and then your mother died and maybe that's when your father's gambling became his secret escape, because all he wanted was one good roll of the dice. And did she like gamblers? Was she drawn to men who take chances? And is that why you feel such a powerful sense of duty to your siblings, because there's always been too much gambling in your family, and somebody's got to bet on a sure thing? What would happen if you let them screw up on their own?

You know you can't prevent tragedy from occurring, right?

So what would happen if you tried to step back and find some wry amusement in your family members' adventures? After all, your family sounds like fun, what with the musicians and hipsters and gamblers. Maybe the story is that when your brother died too, five years after your mom, again the burden fell on your shoulders and again everyone filled with unspeakable grief and confusion but this time your younger sister said to hell with this, I'm going to be a hipster and try to live my life, and your other brother said to hell with this, I'm forming a band and moving to L.A., and your dad said to hell with this, I'm going to the casino. So they all realized they had to just live their lives, and you have been left now as the dutiful one, and it's killing you! So let it go! Maybe if you would only let them all go off and do their sound checks and their raves and play Texas Hold 'em, you would maybe have a few minutes to yourself, and you'd have time for a boyfriend.

You've got to let them go. As the older sibling, you absolutely can abandon your family, at least for one season. In fact, you can make plans right now to spend next holiday season in Mexico. Buy your ticket on your 30th birthday, as a little gift for how good you've been this year.

Should we euthanize the Yorkie?

*My grandmother is ill and cannot care
for her aging Yorkshire terrier.*

Dear Cary,

I AM STRESSED and wrestling with an ethical dilemma: Would it be right to put down the 11-year-old dog of my grandmother, who has middle-onset Alzheimer's disease?

It's the eve of Thanksgiving and my grandparents are both here, with this dog, a tiny, whiny Yorkshire terrier who has learned to beg constantly. It's not her fault; my grandmother forgets that she has just fed her, hears her whine (oh the sound of that whine!) and gives her another largish helping of steak or chicken or cookies, or whatever anyone happens to be eating at the time. As a result, the dog is overweight, out of shape (she will not walk more than five feet before stopping and dragging her feet), largely incontinent (I just wiped up hot dog pee 10 minutes ago), and the most annoying creature on the planet. I mean, I don't have kids yet (I'm 24), but if this were my kid I would send it straight to boarding school.

Unfortunately, though, this dog is the center of my grandmother's small and dimming world, along with my grandfather, who is in fine mental condition but has some cardiac problems—I think she likes to feel that the dog needs her and isn't judging her for mental lapses (not that the rest of the family is, I think we're doing a good job of stimulating and caring for her). My mom asked her once whether she would be more upset if she (her daughter) died or if the dog died, and she indicated that the death of the dog would make her more upset.

But that's what I'm writing to you about. This dog is seriously damaging the fragile universe of care my grandmother has—its incontinence and whininess grate on my poor grandfather, along with the fact that my grandmother refuses to walk the dog or take it outside to go to the bathroom or clean up after it, so it all falls on him. It bothers my aunt, who is the primary caretaker of my grandmother, for mostly the same reasons. They get in screaming fights with my grandmother about it. I know it sounds horrid, but when you combine the stress of caring for an Alzheimer's patient with the stress of caring for a dog who is similarly incapable and needy/whiny, it breaks down the patience and reserve of even the most saintly. I love dogs, but find myself wanting to kick it.

Now it's Thanksgiving, and I will be cooking all day in the kitchen tomorrow. I know the dog will be under my feet, whining incessantly, and yet there's nothing I can do—if I suggest to my grandmother to take it somewhere else (the kitchen is open to the family room where people gather) she will get huffy. Five Thanksgivings ago when something similar happened she started walking home with the dog, two states away, because she was so offended that someone didn't love it as much as she did.

Anyway, there has been some talk of putting the dog down because it is old, incontinent and going blind, and more importantly is breaking down my grandfather's will to live (he's spoken about suicide multiple times) and ability to care for my grandmother. We are pretty sure she would forget about it after a week. No one has yet stepped up to the plate to follow through on this possibility. I'm thinking about it. What do you think? Is it the right or wrong thing to do? Could you live with yourself if you did something similar? Am I sounding as whiny as the dog?

Granddaughter Chef

Dear Granddaughter Chef,

WE CANNOT KILL creatures in our care merely because their illness becomes a problem for the rest of us. We cannot kill the dog for this reason any more than we can kill your grandmother for this reason. Your grandmother and the Yorkie are both creatures in our care. They are not of the same species or the same status. One is a human and one is a dog. But they are both creatures and they both deserve to live.

The Yorkie is overweight and annoying. So are many people we see in the supermarket. That does not mean we get to euthanize them.

There is a place for human death with dignity. There is a place for veterinary euthanasia. The American Veterinary Medical Association published its latest Guidelines on Euthanasia in June 2007. I have just looked through the report, much to the peril of my tranquility. It describes methods mostly. It does not talk about justifications. But it does talk about pain. It talks about the medical reality of pain. Without addressing the ethical question, the focus on pain serves to remind us: The reason to provide an animal with a humane death is to alleviate the animal's pain. Ethically speaking, I think the focus must be on the animal's welfare, not on our own.

You are a recent college graduate and the world will soon be in your care. So I ask you:

What behaviors and attitudes do we wish to cultivate in our society?

This is not an idle question.

The exercise of insouciant power, if given encouragement and room to grow, can become tyranny. The exercise of love and humility, if given encouragement and room to grow, can become benevolence. What benefits our world more, the habit of tyranny or the habit of benevolence?

Why do we not care for our poor in this country? Why do we have no national healthcare? Why do we not house the homeless and feed the hungry? Why are we a culture of convenience rather than of service? Why on a holiday like Thanksgiving do we turn to the question of whether to kill the dog?

Is it because, to risk the tautological, that is who we are?

So who are we? Who we are is bounded by the unthinkable. So what is unthinkable? Consider: If it were unthinkable for a member of Congress to propose that we not give medicine to the sick, that we leave the moneyless and the jobless to live in the streets, then anyone who proposed such a thing would be shunned, no? If it were unthinkable, then any person who proposed policies that led to citizens being left to shit in alleyways and to lie on filthy blankets in front of opulent storefronts would be shunned, right? If it were unthinkable to have such a world, would not anyone who proposed such policies be condemned as a barbarian?

But it is not unthinkable. It is not unthinkable at all. It is the policy of this nation to leave large numbers of its citizens without care.

So if that is not unthinkable, then what is unthinkable in our world? What is beyond the pale? And what, therefore, by inference, do we most deeply honor?

It is beyond the pale to criticize our soldiers.

At this moment, having uttered those words "our soldiers," it is customary to insert a pious disclaimer, pledging the highest respect for our men and women in uniform. Why? Why have we become a society in which any mention of our soldiers must include an honorific? What has changed about our country that we must now explicitly state our highest respect for the individual men and women in uniform any time we mention them? Has anyone noticed that the obligatory inclusion of an honorific has chilling historical and cultural echoes?

And why is it beyond the pale to criticize soldiers but not beyond the pale to criticize professors? If we honored knowledge as highly as we honor killing, would it not be grounds for censure in the halls of Congress for a congressman to vilify a professor, a philosopher, a poet or novelist?

What else can one conclude? We do not honor knowledge. We honor killing.

Is it any surprise then that the first solution that comes to mind to the problem of the annoying and overweight Yorkie is to kill it?

We cannot do this. We cannot kill out of mere convenience.

So what to do? You mention only four people in your letter: Your grandmother, grandfather, mother and aunt. But there must be other family and friends who might be willing to help in such a situation. So what I suggest is that you go to your aunt and you say, "The dog is not getting adequate care here. We must find adequate care for the dog." Make getting adequate care for the dog a high priority, a must-do.

There are two ways to provide adequate care for the dog. Either have someone care for the dog at home, or have the dog live somewhere else. If your aunt is caring for your grandmother, perhaps she can also care for the dog. If no one in the house can adequately care for the dog, however, it would be best for the dog to live somewhere else and occasionally be brought over to visit your grandmother. There must be a dog lover somewhere among your family's friends and acquaintances. It would be an act of charity and love if someone would take care of the dog in its last years. Look into the local culture of animal lovers. Look into Yorkie Rescue (but beware of the audio!). There must be someone who can take care of this dog.

One final thing. You say that the dog has broken down your grandfather's will to live. If your grandfather is having suicidal thoughts, that is a matter to be referred to a social worker and/or a therapist. It is not the dog's fault. The dog is part of the situation. The dog is part of the family. But the situation is much bigger than that.

In other words, let's not blame it on the dog.

It's gift-giving time, and
I'm cranky about gift cards
and pushy kids

It used to be so much fun to pick out the perfect gift.
Now it seems kids just want the cash.

Dear Cary,

I NEED A little help with perspective. I would like to get some philosophical guidance and your thoughts on gift giving.

It's not life-and-death stuff, but it has my stomach in knots as I do my Christmas shopping. It affects my relationship with family members and the fun of the holidays more every year.

I am getting really cranky about gift cards.

I have a large family, and we all have spouses and most have kids. Every year my parents and brothers and sisters and spouses draw names and have a moderate $75 limit for that one gift. The children do not draw names and receive gifts from every family. Now, it's hard to keep up with everyone's changing likes and dislikes and hobbies and interests, so for convenience and fun my mom has always had a big list on her fridge where we had individual lists of suggestions and wishes. We always had a good time adding outlandish things to each other's lists, and it also came in handy when I was stumped for my own husband or kids.

However, in recent years, many of the lists have deteriorated to a litany of gift cards from only the hottest stores. The latest trend, even more detestable to me, is to state what the person does not want! As in,

"No tea or candles, or toys or dresses or sweaters—pants, [blah-blah] designer only, please" or, "No books. Tiffany will never read them." Is this what the idea of gift giving in our time has become?

But maybe I'm the Scrooge. Am I the Scrooge, Cary? What is it that bothers me here? I mean, now I can just go down to the convenience store on the corner and do all my holiday shopping from one of those spinny things near the cash register—all the different cards are there. Or better yet, why don't we just stop at the ATM on Christmas Day on our way to Mom and Dad's and exchange wads of cash?

I guess what I feel is robbed. I loved thinking of the perfect gift—the one my sister would never get herself or the great surprise my brother hadn't even thought of...I liked looking for clothes for my nieces in that locally owned store in the funky part of town...buying a book for my nephew that my son loved as a boy...I feel robbed of the feeling of giving. Some people will say, "Just do what you want, and still give in the way that you want to." But the giving is really tainted, knowing that what they'd really like is a plastic swipe card. The reaction I get is that the recipient is annoyed with my gift rather than pleased. It may seem frivolous, but it makes me really sad.

A number of years ago I read Miss Manners or Emily Post (or someone like that), who said that gifts should always be accepted graciously and enthusiastically. She even went so far as to say that returns and exchanges should be done only if they could be done discreetly and without the gift giver's knowledge. Incidentally, she was also in favor of regifting (once again discreetly). This feels right to me and SO FAR from where we're at in our consumer holiday traditions. What do you think?

Please help me find some perspective.

Maybe Scrooge

Dear Maybe Scrooge,

SAY WHAT YOU will about the decline of civility, kids adapt to the situation they find themselves in. Kids today, what situation do they find themselves in? They find themselves in an indescribably opulent, decadent, end-of-the-world orgy of cheap luxury goods. The threat they face is not that maybe they won't get what they want, but that they'll be buried under an avalanche of merchandise like the good people of Pompeii. What are they supposed to do about this?

Well, they develop their defensive capacities. They learn to discriminate among the objects. They learn the language that the postmodern brand maniacs are speaking to them, and they learn to speak it back. Amid a surfeit of middle-class consumer goods and a fragmented sensorium of image and sound never before seen on earth, they develop a preternatural radar for brand recognition. It's a survival adaptation. It's like they're in this postmodern Jurassic Park of predatory marketers running social-networking sites and gaming geniuses baiting their traps with neurological candy. What are they supposed to do? They didn't invent this world. They're not responsible. We are, you and I, actively or passively, with our acquiescence in this late capitalist supernova imperialist explosion, our cathode-ray image strafing of tender minds, our Facebook surveillance of inner space, our giant data-mining tractors running up and down their streets sucking up their every movie preference and snack preference, our "South Park" boot camp of social toughening scouring out any last sentimental vestiges of modernist depth-model identity.

We made this world. It is a pretty amazing world, with its weapons and pixels. It's an amazing killing machine; it's an amazing mechanism of domination and control; it is amazing in its surveillance capabilities and its persuasion techniques.

But to a kid it's got to be mainly a terrifying world.

They're programmed, like all other humans, to scan their environment, find the patterns, find the survival strategies and gather goods. So they have responded to their environment in an intelligent and reasonable way, by becoming discriminating shoppers. They scan merchandise with virtuosic speed and exactitude. They mentally sort, scan, sort, scan, discriminate, sort, prioritize, pick the next top model, the next American Idol.

Where, I ask you, are they supposed to find the values that you are talking about? Sure, parents can try to teach them these things. But kids look at their parents, and then they look at the world, and they go, What the fuck? They see the toys spewing out of the world's vast maws of plastic-mold technology, they see the microchips doubling in speed and know that in a year they will be faster and faster still, and tinier and tinier still, and more feature-rich too. They see the new dresses and the new videos, and they know they'll be changing faster than they can change their own clothes. And then they look at their parents, who seem to be moving in black-and-white slo-mo. How can they feel anything but pity and scorn? How can they have any confidence that their parents will even survive the acceleration? In fact it must frighten them that their parents seem so ill-adapted to the world that parents themselves have created.

And then we come along and we say, "I'm knitting you a sweater and I want you to be grateful for it." And they think, Are you out of your head? Are you nuts? Do you have any idea what's going on in the world?

Of course you do, and of course it terrifies you, too. You are only trying to hold onto something, some shred of the world as it used to be before it started spinning so fast.

I don't blame you. But these kids are the ones who are going to have to live in this world. So if they can find any comforting illusions in it, more power to them. And if they are a little rude and a little acquisitive and a little overattuned to the minute variations in brand identities, if they want only the cash, if they dismiss our offers of hand-knit sweaters and perfect picture books, well, I'd say they have bigger things to worry about. For instance, I didn't even mention this: We're handing down to them a planet that has been overheating lately and whose warranty has expired.

So if you want to get to know these kids better, I'd say let them take you shopping.

As for the future of the world, they're going to have to make it for themselves. God help them on that one.

My married boyfriend's ditching me for Christmas

He's going home to his family without me.
Could that be because we're both still hitched?

Dear Cary,

I'VE BEEN IN a committed, monogamous relationship for a year and a half. My boyfriend's family lives out of state, although I met his mom when she visited over the summer. Each of us is currently separated although still technically married to our exes.

About a week ago my boyfriend informed me that he'd be going away for Christmas to spend the week with his mom and siblings. While I understand the desire to visit with family during the holiday season, I feel forlorn and bereft that his leaving means I'm on my own. I'm also a little ticked off that it didn't occur to him to wonder about what I'd be doing for Christmas, and when I brought it up he said truthfully that it never occurred to him to include me.

Look, I get it. He doesn't want to bring me home with him, he's still technically married, as am I, and it's scary to bring a new girl home. But a year and a half, dude—I'm not that new anymore!

Cary, am I just dating the world's most self-centered guy? I love him a lot, and he's usually pretty considerate—very giving in bed, etc.—but it seems that the holidays are a big blind spot for him and he has no idea why this is upsetting me. I've tried talking to him about it, but, hey, if he really doesn't care about my feelings (as evidenced by his lack of forethought when making his plans), I don't think my whining about it is going to make him care any more, or treat me with any better consideration.

What should I do? I can suck it up and make other holiday plans with friends, but it's going to be a blue Christmas without him. Also, I worry that if we don't resolve this, my resentment could fester indefinitely, ruining the pretty sweet thing we have now.

Lonesome Stocking Stuffer

Dear Stocking Stuffer,

YOU ASK WHETHER his action indicates that he is self-centered. I think it indicates that he has taken other people into consideration. It's just that those other people are not you. Those other people are his family.

Think of it from his perspective. He's married. His family knows he's married. They may not be so thrilled with the fact that he's separated from his wife and dating someone new.

His mother met you, but you aren't her daughter-in-law. Think of it from her perspective. She may have had great hopes for her son's marriage. She may have loved her daughter-in-law. So then the news comes that her son's marriage is in trouble.

Families take marriage seriously is what I'm saying. To them it's not just a technicality. It's a matter of the heart, and also of the family's collective economic security. They get their hopes up. They go to a wedding, they see their son stand up there and take solemn vows, their hearts fill with ideas about what the future might be, about what their grandkids might look like, about how they might spend the next 30 or 40 years together, how they might grow to love their daughter-in-law.

Then comes word that the marriage isn't working out. OK, so they feel some disappointment. Comes word that he has moved out, that they'll probably get divorced. OK, but they're not divorced yet.

So if the son shows up at Christmas time with his new girlfriend, who is also still married, maybe it puts a little tension on the family. Here's this new person they don't know, and they're supposed to behave...how? Like they think it's perfectly OK for their still-married son to show up at the house with his new girlfriend, who is also still married? Don't you think they'd feel awkward?

So if I were you I would be glad that your boyfriend is a thoughtful person who is capable of thinking of his family and their feelings.

You'll miss your boyfriend over Christmas. It's unfortunate. But there are other people to consider.

So make some plans with your friends. Have a good time.

If I were you, I'd be glad that your boyfriend made the decision he did. He certainly could have handled it more gently. But he's doing the right thing. Maybe if you can see it this way, you can spend your Christmas free of the notion that he doesn't care about you. Of course he cares about you. But he also cares about his family—enough to put their feelings first.

Visiting my family gets me down

Every time I see them I'm depressed for a week

Dear Cary,

FIRST, THANK YOU for being persistent with your crazy wisdom, and for not giving up. I enjoy your column.

I need a new way to think about this situation, and I'm hoping you can help. Here is a bit of background, in case it helps.

I live in a separate state from my family, and visit about five or six times per year. My relationship with my parents was dicey for a long time, but it is now more even, as I started simultaneously sticking up for myself more, and caring about their approval less. I'm in my mid-30s now. After a wandering employment history (two different careers), I am now underemployed in some ways, but happy to have a job, and try to be useful. Married, have some pets that I adore. I have a history of depression but am managing for the most part. No children because I spent a long time not feeling good, and now that I feel more OK, I don't want to ruin it (not that I dislike children, I just want some internal peace and am too old to have a bit of peace and then have children).

My problem is that every time I visit my family, I feel like shit for three to four days afterward. I don't feel bad while I'm there (anymore). In fact, things are better than they've ever been. But this shitty feeling, it is on the inside, and it takes me days to shake it off, even when I try to talk myself into a better place. I try to get at exactly what this feeling is about, and the most I can tell is that I feel like a loser when I'm there. It's kind of an extension of the more pervasive feeling

I have that I somehow just don't fit in, that there is something slightly "off" about me.

The strange thing is, my parents aren't all that successful or well adjusted. If anything, I'm slightly more adjusted than they are, unless I just have no objectivity and am fooling myself. My sister and her husband are more successful in that they both have careers and a more standard life, by American standards. When I ask myself if I'm jealous, I am not so much envious of their standard lives as I am of their seeming feeling of "fitting in." In other words, I don't necessarily want what they have (my parents and my sibling), but I want to feel like they feel. This is true not only of my family, but of society in general—I don't really admire the lifestyle I'm told I should want, but I want the part of the dream that has me feeling good about myself. It's just, for some reason, that this part that I lack is more pronounced when I'm with my family.

Anyway, I do not want to stop seeing my family. They're basically good people. But this does affect my willingness to visit for extended periods, since it is really inconvenient to feel shitty for a week afterward. I'm embarrassed that I still feel this way well into my 30s. Is there anything I can do about this, or is this just how it is?

Confused

Dear Confused,

YOUR FAMILY IS never going to be the family you wish you had and they are never going to give you the feeling you wish they would give you and you are never going to fit in the way you wish you fit in and the sooner you realize this and get angry about it and shout it out and bang your fists on the floor and scream at the gods about it and grieve it and fully accept it and let it go the sooner you can be at peace with yourself and your gifts and the way you are loved now.

The way you are now is the way you are loved. Those who love you do not love this other person you wish you were. They do not even know who that person is. The way you are now is the way you are loved.

You think there is some other person you might be if you were only different but even if she showed up on your doorstep you wouldn't know who she is because she would be lacking the full code of you. There is only one person who has the full code of you. There is only one person who can be loved as you and it is your job to keep being that person.

Why are you sad after being with your family? Because you start pretending to be somebody else because you think somebody else deserves their love. And then you lose your bearings. It takes days to put yourself back together. So remember:

It is you whom the people who love you love. They don't need you to pretend. When you pretend they just wait for you to come back.

(Here is one reason I am a writer and not a therapist: If I were a therapist I would start making stuff up just to have something new to say. So I will not say for the umpteenth time to read "Feeling Good" by Dr. David Burns even though you probably should read it anyway because it seems to help with things like this.)

To sense that your family does not really love or approve of you hurts but it doesn't mean you're supposed to be somebody else. It means you're supposed to bear that sadness with dignity; it means you're supposed to bear that loss as a wise person would, knowing it's just the tension between your capacity for dreaming and your capacity for acceptance.

Some people are fine because they don't think about the infinite possibilities but some of us do think about the infinite possibilities which would be fine if that were all we did but then we also think about how much it sucks that these infinite possibilities do not all come to fruition although if you think about it there must be a natural cap on the number of infinite possibilities that are brought into being just as there must be a finite number of partners at Goldman Sachs.

You are here to do the one job no one else can do and that job is to fulfill the destiny written on your skin in a place you cannot read without turning inside out. Take several deep breaths. Stop what you are doing.

What is the source of your sadness?

Do I have the right to control how Christmas money is used?

Last year I sent my brother a check to buy gifts for his kids, and he spent it on a video game.

Dear Cary,

WITH CHRISTMAS COMING I am faced with the dilemma of what to do for my nephews. My family has opted out of gift giving among adults, but we want the boys—ages 7 and 3—to enjoy the holiday with all the magic a visit from Santa brings.

My problem is this. My brother is terrible with money. We are complete opposites in that I save an appropriate percentage of my income and have no debt, while he is deep in consumer debt and always looking for another expensive item to finance.

Last year I sent him a check so he could buys gifts for the boys from me. We live on opposite coasts, and rather than guess sizes and interests, it made more sense in my mind for the parents to do the shopping. Yet when I asked what the large check was used for, my brother replied with a vague story about spending the money on a video game. (Apparently the most expensive video game in the history of thumb blisters.) The only logical conclusion was that he had spent the money elsewhere—and not on the boys.

This year I decided to work instead with my sister-in-law. While I don't know her well enough to determine how much better (or worse) she is with finances, I know her dedication to the boys' education. Therefore, I sent an e-mail to her, asking what educational store she would like a Christmas gift certificate from so that she could purchase instructional materials. I now await her response.

My question is this. Is it appropriate for me to ask that they spend the Christmas money I provide on a gift of my choosing—or at least for the children? Or, if I'm that invested in having the money spent wisely, should I do my own shopping for the boys, knowing I may not get them the best gifts possible?

I ask that you not lose the question in pontification about our family. We aren't close. I'm not up-to-date on the children's every runny nose and spelling test—and that won't change. No amount of admonishment will bring about a Very Brady Christmas, so save the tut-tut-tut.

This is purely about whether it is appropriate to have expectations of money I provide, or if that right is lost once the cash is gifted.

Thank you for your thoughts.

Nest Egg

Dear Nest Egg,

I THINK YOU ought to pick out gifts yourself and send them to the kids. That solves the whole problem right there.

If upon further consideration you would like additional pontification I am willing to provide it at no additional cost.

Until then, rest assured, you'll hear no tut-tut-tutting from me.

Have a Christmas.

Please, Mom, please:
Not another dress shirt!

Every year for 30 years she sends me the same thing for Christmas. Will it ever end?

Dear Cary,

I COULD MAKE this a very long letter, with many examples of puzzling (disturbing?) behavior on the part of my wealthy parents, who are still going strong as 80-somethings, but I'm not going to. Instead, I'm going to ask you about one particular behavior that I am hoping will act like a Rosetta stone, allowing me to translate all of their other, um, "interesting" behaviors into a language I can understand. I myself am pushing 50 and not doing very well. Underemployed, alone, trust issues, depressed (too working poor for anything remotely resembling insurance or disposable income, so please don't suggest counseling), etc.

So here it is: Every single Christmas my mother gives me a dress shirt and a tie. Thirty years ago I had a job for which I had to dress nicely. The shirts got worn, even though like many guys I hate getting clothes as a gift. (Give me a gadget!) For years I said, "Please don't get me a shirt. I don't wear them, I don't need them." And yet, every single year there it is in its predictable rectangular box (though to be fair, sans tie for the last decade or so). I have a stack of shirts, still in their boxes. I finally gave up. Still, the shirts come. Recently, my sister even told my mom not to get me a shirt. Still, they come. What's up with that? Why would a parent insist on giving their child something he has repeatedly told them he doesn't want and doesn't need? And particularly, if my mom has a narcissistic personality disorder as I suspect (all signs point to Rome), what does this behavior mean?

Not Another Shirt, Please

Dear Not Another Shirt,

THE THING ABOUT truly self-absorbed people is that often the presents they give you are burdens for you to carry or tasks for you to perform. Here is a lovely umbrella. Now hold it over me as I walk. Here is a lovely shirt. You do not like it? That does not matter. You are only a reflection of me.

It is customary for all sorts of parents, not just the terribly self-absorbed, to mark holidays by choosing a commercially available object of relative anonymity (something whose utility though limited is also unquestioned and whose applicability to one's own life though marginal cannot be utterly disproved—who, for instance, does not wear socks?) and wrapping it in colorful paper, packaging it in sturdy cardboard and placing it in the hands of a uniformed courier who deposits it in a mailbox or on a doorstep, quietly and anonymously, like a tooth fairy leaving a coin under your pillow while you sleep.

If the parents are very busy people, they may employ not only a courier but some kind of secretarial help to choose the objects and make sure no holiday is overlooked. The wealthy and self-absorbed parent, intent on wasting as little time as possible on others, might find it attractive to automate or outsource the entire process. So your mother, while having initially decided that your annual gift would be a shirt, may not even be aware, at her age, that this process she set into motion long ago continues with such absurd repetitiveness.

Nonetheless, the objects one chooses can be quite revealing.

The shirt is the sartorial equivalent of the face, while the pants are the sartorial equivalent of the body. The shirt is pride, money, position; the pants are vigor, authority, power. When we talk of power we talk of who wears the pants; when we talk of money we talk of losing the shirt. The shirt is also about self-control and status.

So by sending you a shirt your mother may be saying, Maintain control, maintain your place in society, go out and get a job, make something of yourself—a magical incantation repeated yearly so that you will not degenerate into a raving, shirtless man.

If she is narcissistic, she only says it because you reflect poorly on her. If she is as self-involved as you indicate, the yearly shirt may only be an infuriating diversion from the fact of her lifelong neglect.

But the fact that you protest and never wear the shirt is beside the point: The point is that she knows her son has a clean shirt and thus need never leave the warm embrace of your social class. You may be the penniless remittance man, disappointment to all, shivering in shamefully reduced circumstances but possessed always of this one necessity: A clean shirt.

Perhaps you wish she would finally give you something truly of herself—that is what the self-absorbed do to us, they taunt us, they tempt us, they fill us with hunger. But most likely you must content yourself with this routine annual inscription on the cold heavens: a shirt for Christmas, commemorating a miraculous birth. In fact, perhaps every Christmas she feels an ancient twinge at the torment your arrival caused her, as, she issued you into the world—shirtless.

I'm a soldier in Iraq— how about a card or letter from home?

I've asked my family to write but they say they're too busy.

Dear Cary,

HAPPY HOLIDAYS; HOPE this letter finds you well. I've been reading your column for a long time and respect your advice, so I'm seeking some of it here. The brass tacks of it: I'm deployed in Iraq and I'm depressed as all hell. I would love nothing more this holiday than a card from my family or loved ones, something, anything, and here it is late December, and nothing. I try and talk to my family about this, but every time I go to bring it up I feel like a selfish ass or am reminded how busy everyone is. Help me out, man, am I being a selfish ass? Trust me, I can certainly take a yes and any advice you may have to see another view.

Thanks,
Benjamin

Dear Benjamin,

I FORWARDED YOUR note to your family. Their response was rather surprising:

Dear Benjamin,

How selfish of you!

    Sure, you are getting shot at, having bombs go off in your cafeteria, driving over explosive devices, having your deployment extended with no end in sight, blah blah blah. But don't you realize that we, too, face dangers every day? Who knows when the Internet connection could go down and the whole family can't log on! Who knows when the newspaper might not arrive, and somebody might have to drive to 7-Eleven and buy the paper—and then: Are you still expected to give the paperboy a tip, or what?

    There are phone calls to make, Benjamin—important phone calls to friends and not just to any friends either but to close friends— friends of a kind of closeness that you and your buddies, with your silly risking your lives for each other, wouldn't know anything about! And there are gifts to wrap and give to each other—did you think all these gifts we're giving to each other just wrap themselves? Cards and gifts. Stuff for each other. That's what we're busy with. Why haven't you received any? Maybe because you're way over there in Iraq. Do you know how far that is? Do you know how inconvenient it's been for us to have to look on a map to see where you are—I mean a big map, the kind that goes beyond Rockaway Beach?

    Why did you have to go over there in the first place? Don't you think the world's problems would have worked themselves out eventually? But no. You had to go enlist, protect the country, be of service, live by a code of honor, blah blah blah yadda yadda yadda.

    Besides, Benjamin, how can we be thinking of you when you never drop by? Do you expect us to remember you exist when we don't see you for week after week? Now, if you were living next door like our junior life and casualty underwriter for Northwestern Life (you think life and you think casualty but this is life and casualty!) or pursuing a graduate degree in the metaphysics of silicone breast implants or trying to start up your own reality TV show like some cousins we know, maybe you'd be a little more in touch.

    But don't worry, we forgive you. Silly Benjamin, always trying to help. Anyway, we've heard it gets very hot there in the summer, but it's winter now, isn't it? Maybe they'll give you an extra blanket but don't make a pest of yourself. And for God's sake, no matter what you do, don't let them see you shivering in the cold the way you used to when you were a little boy!

Love,
Your Family

Well, Benjamin, I just made that up. I thought it might make you chuckle, and I figured you could use a chuckle. But seriously I wanted to tell you that most of us over here are awed by the sacrifices you are making on our behalf. We are capable of making the distinction between policies we disagree with and our countrymen and women who are carrying them out. I know that's two ideas to hold in your head at one time, but we can handle it. So for you and all the other soldiers over there whose families are too busy this holiday season: We all love you and care about you back home, and we are deeply humbled by the fact that you're laying your lives on the line so that we can go on watching television, talking on the phone and buying stuff that doesn't make our butts look big.

We'll never be able to thank you enough, so, frankly, we probably won't. You'll just have to know that it's true: In our hearts, we appreciate it more than we can say.

Readers: Want to send this poor soldier boy a letter? Send to advice@salon.com via your own mail program, making sure "To the Soldier" is in the subject line. I'll forward your mail along to him sometime before midnight on Christmas Eve. That might cheer him up a bit, no?

Update on the lonely soldier

Remember that soldier in Iraq sitting all by himself wishing the family would write? Response from readers was amazing.

Dear Cary,

COULD YOU PLEASE give us an update on the poor soldier who was alone at Christmas with the family that was "too busy" to write? Did you get many responses from readers for him?

Brenda

Dear Brenda,

WOW. DID I get many responses? Yes, it was amazing. All told, more than 400 readers were moved enough by that soldier's letter to write to him. I've been meaning to update everybody on that. Here's what happened:

I was on vacation on Friday, Dec. 24, the day the soldier's column was on the cover. I happened to check my e-mail and saw this note: "Cary, why don't you set up a Hotmail (or something) account for that soldier, give him the password, and then publish the address so this poor guy can get greetings from your readers? It might not happen in time for Christmas, but it probably could for New Year's and he would love it, I'm sure."

That seemed like a pretty good idea, I said to my wife. However, it would require getting in touch with the soldier, whose whereabouts I didn't know, getting his OK, setting up the account, getting the password to him, then publishing it. As I considered all the steps involved, I decided to take a simpler, if more labor-intensive, route and just publish a notice in that day's column inviting readers to send greetings to the soldier at the advice@salon e-mail address, and I would forward them. I published that notice on the column around midday Dec. 24.

Then my wife and I went about our business. We wrapped presents, we cooked some food, and then set off to see the "Nutcracker" with niece, nephew and in-laws, as we traditionally do on Xmas Eve. (Tradition also dictates that every year we forget to make reservations at any restaurant, preferring instead the holiday cheer of wandering chilly San Francisco with hungry children in tow, looking for a place to eat. It seemed that every place we might eat was either closed or full. Incredibly, both Max's Opera Cafe and Chevy's were closed! John's Grill was full up. The Hayes Street Grill was full up. But wait! What's this! Caffe delle Stelle has a corner table in the window! For six! There is a restaurant God after all!)

After dinner we came home and toasted marshmallows in the fireplace and opened presents. (I got a furry jacket, which I am now wearing all the time.) After Dom and Doris and the kids left, the fire was dying down, and it was quiet and warm in the house and I was alone with my wife, and it seemed like an ideal time to...check my e-mail!

That was our "It's a Wonderful Life" moment: The letters had been pouring in all afternoon and evening! It was so sweet! It was so moving! There were hundreds of letters—thoughtful, kind, measured letters recognizing the simple fact that, policy differences be damned, this guy is family. So we spent the rest of Christmas Eve forwarding these letters to that soldier. Here are some of the things that people said:

Gaaahhh, your letter in Salon was terrible! From at least the 15 people I told this to, Happy Freaking Holiday!! A thousand smooches from the pretty girls. A thousand pats on the back from the boys.

Aw, c'mon, Cary, give us saps out here a way to contact poor Benjamin and his guys there in Iraq so we can send them letters and cards and homemade body armor and stuff.

Thank you for laying your life on the line for the rest of us back home. Thank you for enduring life in Iraq.

I propose that your family is ultimately too distracted by the culture they live in to see past the crap that burdens their existence. It's what we all do—define ourselves by the norms and expectations of our culture. So I cannot believe they don't love you and wish you were with them, and maybe they're also quietly terrified of having you where you are.

Mahalo, Mele Kalikimaka and Hauoli Makahiki Hou from Hilo, HI!

I was and am against the war, but I have tremendous respect for people like you who are willing to put your lives on the line for this country, regardless of my feelings (or yours) about the decisions made by the political leadership.

Those are just a few quotes from the first few letters. Reading through them still gives me some kind of chill. I don't know what it is. I guess it's just plain old goodness and compassion and decency is what it is.

My wife and I sat there at the iMac and forwarded as many letters as we could by midnight, and then we went to bed.

I got a quick note from him the next morning, saying, "Merry Christmas, brother, and my most sincere thanks to everyone who has replied."

Not too long afterward, I got another, longer note from him:

Dear Cary,

MY WIFE IS also a regular Salon reader, it didn't take long after she read the letter for her to put two and two together and immediately hit me up. We talked for hours over I.M. and I think both of us were reduced to uncontrollable sobbing through it all. She apologized profusely and passed the word onto my family, who also in turn have responded in droves. Sometimes a kick in the pants is all that's needed to remind us of the truly important things in life.

I don't want anyone to get the wrong impression. This deployment has been extremely hard on my wife, who has had to deal with severe financial constraints; I'm in the National Guard, and we took a severe pay cut when I deployed, raising our son, trying to keep everything on the home front secure and all the things a spouse does when their partner heads off to foreign lands.

Thank you, Cary. Thank you for your words of advice and for all of your readers who have responded with all their love and support. It means the world to so many of us over here, so far away from those we love and care for.

All my love to you and your readers,

Benjamin

Pretty cool, huh?

My family gives me no respect

*I'm accomplished and responsible
but they treat me like a loser.*

Dear Cary,

I HAVE A great job, own my own home, car, dog and medium-size 401K, have put myself through college and law school. I am not a loser! So why does my whole family treat me like one?

My family is not a normal set of folks; we are in a whole new category of dysfunctional and it would take 20 hours' worth of couch time to even come close to describing the crazy things below the surface. Anyway, the issue is that I want to be loved and respected. I am loved by some but respect is just not there.

My youngest sister is forever telling me how poor my judgment is, how bad my understanding of people is and how unprofessional I am, despite the evidence of my high-powered job at an internationally renowned organization. I have a résumé to die for. That is not just a boast but a statement of fact (OK, a boast, too. I need to bolster myself since I am not getting it from outside sources). She tells me that she has no faith in me, in my judgment or in anything about me, that my house is awful, my neighborhood sucks, my dog is poorly trained, etc. And this is the sister I get along with best.

My mother makes it clear that a woman of 39 (me) without a husband and without children is a loser by definition. I had a husband, a drug-abusing, foul-mouthed yet charming brute who almost bankrupted me, stole from me and my friends, cheated on me with other women and possibly men, and verbally abused me in public and private. Dumping him after seven years of marriage was the best decision of my life. I feel lucky that any of my self-esteem survived that one. Yet, here we are five years later and my mother still criticizes me for not keeping that guy! Her current advice: Find a man who wants American citizenship and trade my bed for a green card!

My father barely speaks to me because I dated a guy he did not like a year ago. Two of my sisters do not speak to me at all. I honestly do not know why but both claim to be angry at me. My brother thinks I am an irresponsible idiot. My last sister, who is the only one who acknowledges me as a fully grown and responsible adult, still tells me that my divorce from an abusive ex is a sign of my inability to keep a commitment!

For God's sake, what is it going to take to get these people to admit that I am fine as I am and why the hell do I care! Are these people overly judgmental or am I insane?

Dissed by My Family,

Dear Dissed,

YOU ARE FINE as you are. I know that. You know that. It's the truth.

But your family is never going to give you what you want. That's also the truth.

You will never be at peace with your family until you stop wanting what they will never give you.

It is easy to say, "Accept the way things are."

But exactly how do we accept things? What is this action called acceptance? I would say that acceptance is knowing rather than wishing. You studied law. You committed many laws to memory. You may wish they were one way but they are the way they are. If you go into the courtroom and expect the laws to be different from the way they are you will not succeed. You must accept that the law is the way it is. You must know the law.

The same is true with your family. You must know your family as it is. You must study your family and know it thoroughly. That is your route to acceptance. Regard your family as a fact, immutable as the law. They are what they are. They behave in a certain way. The facts are unpleasant. But they are facts.

What happens to people who do not like the law and so do not obey it? They get their asses kicked.

You may not like what you know about your family but you must accept it or you will get your ass kicked. You will step into the ring expecting a kiss and get slapped. Don't do it. Don't let them kick you around.

You may find it hard to accept your family as it is. There are reasons for that. One reason is that in accepting your family as it is, you have to give up, or mourn, the ideal family that never was. You may have to go through a sort of grieving process. You may have to feel the hurt, the lifelong ache of wanting a family that is loving and kind and supportive and never getting it. It hurts. It hurts a lot. It hurts for a long time. But that is the price of knowing the truth.

I think the truth is worth it.

Here is a consolation: This other family, this ideal, imaginary family that you always wanted, this family that really gets you, that supports you, that appreciates you as you appreciate yourself: It is a real family, too. It is real in your mind. You can keep it, in fact. You can keep this imaginary family in your mind. This dream family is your family, too. It's the family you deserve. It lives on a different street in a different neighborhood where only you can go.

Here is another consolation. Sometimes if you leave something alone long enough it begins to heal on its own and one day long after you have given up even thinking about it a gift arrives in the mail that is so delightful you break down right there on your doorstep because you had given up all hope of such a thing ever, ever happening.

I'm just saying it's possible. Maybe one day if you leave this alone it may fix itself. But don't hold your breath. Let it be.

Your family today is sad and difficult and dangerous. Remember that. Accept it. Don't give them the opportunity to kick you around anymore.

Get what you need some other way. Get it from people who have it to give.

Holiday heartaches

*My ex—who broke up with me two months ago—
will probably be at a New Year's party I want to attend.
Should I go and risk seeing him?*

Dear Cary,

I MOVED TO Europe seven months ago to get my Ph.D. Two months ago, my boyfriend of five years broke up with me over the telephone, saying that the distance was too hard and that our relationship "wasn't worth the effort." I have not had contact with him since the breakup, and have been focused on working through this.

I will be visiting the U.S. for Christmas, and would like to attend the annual New Year's Eve party my ex-boyfriend and I both traditionally attend. The hostess has said that my comfort and happiness are a priority and if I wish, my ex will not be invited. My dilemma is that my ex would not require an invitation to attend. I don't know if I am ready to see him or talk to him, but I do know I'm not prepared to do so at a party.

I've considered that the simplest solution would be to not attend the party, but it is an opportunity to see many people I have no other possibility to see. Is it appropriate for me to mail him a letter requesting he not attend? Should I see him at all? I'm not ready to have a friendship with him yet, and I'm not interested in updating each other on our lives. I would be willing to see him if it would facilitate my healing process.

Need Your Insight

Dear Need Your Insight,

IF HE WAS a really classy guy, he might let the hostess know that because he'd broken up with you, he was not attending; and the hostess would then tell you he would not be attending.

But let's assume he's not all that classy a guy.

So let's say, best-case scenario, you get to town a couple of days before the party and go see him, not to discuss anything, just to lay eyes on him to find out what it feels like to lay eyes on him. That way you can go to the party knowing what it feels like to lay eyes on him, so you're not distracted by anticipation of that moment.

Bottom line, regardless: You're going to the party. Things like that are so important: traditions, your friends. For you to triumph over this little social obstacle is important too, I think—not to be cowed or robbed of an experience that belongs to you.

I don't think it's a good idea to ask him not to attend, or to ask the hostess not to invite him. If you ask him not to attend, you're giving him power over your fate. Don't give him that power. Deal with it yourself, if he's there or not there.

So do the courageous, classy thing and show up at the party regardless of what he does. If he's there, just don't pay him any mind. Act with some dignity and cool.

Let him be the one who's nervous.

Oh, here's the other thing: You say it's a New Year's Eve party. Isn't that the party where everybody gets drunk and kisses each other? If I were you, for just this New Year's Eve, I would stay sober. I'm not saying I think getting drunk on New Year's Eve is a bad thing. But this is one year where you need to pull this one off with coolness, control and dignity.

I'm having a
European family feud

*Our last visit to my family in Europe erupted
in acrimony among the siblings.*

Dear Cary,

FOR THE LAST 19 years, my husband and I have lived in the east-
ern U.S., across the Atlantic from my family. My two older siblings
and my parents live within several miles of each other in the same
European capital. It's an arrangement that's worked quite well for me
because I find my family a bit overpowering at times.

Recently, though, the distance has been causing problems. This
last Christmas, we traveled over there, taking our 6-year-old son and
1-year-old daughter. It was the first time we'd crossed the Atlantic
with the baby, and we found the combination of jet lag and baby-
related sleep deprivation crushing. We were staying with my parents
(they're the only ones with a spare room) and it's fair to say that we
weren't always gracious guests, especially in the first week (we stayed
for three). All things considered, though, I thought we did OK.

A couple of days before we came back to the States, though, my
sister and brother sat me down for a talk. They'd decided it was no
longer appropriate for me and my family to stay with our parents
when we visit. Our father, who's now 81, is not in great health and
they feel it's too much of a strain for him to have us in the house. My
brother offered to help us find a sublet or house swap for our next
visit, and I agreed.

Then the conversation turned to my husband. They had complaints about his behavior. He's aloof. He's not a family person. He doesn't ask them questions about themselves. My brother has been harping on this theme to me, on and off, for a few years. I've told him to go directly to my husband if he has a problem because I figure, why should I be the messenger? This time, he actually did go to my husband. And the result was horrible. My husband felt attacked, got defensive and basically told my brother to f--- off. This made my brother even angrier than before.

We left under a cloud, with everyone feeling crappy. Then things got worse. I wrote an e-mail to my sister saying I was upset about the sudden attack on my husband. In response, she wrote me a long letter eloquently describing what she saw as MY character flaws. She held no punches and was very cruel. To quote one example: "It seems that you insist upon holding on to every perceived slight against you in a self-destructive way that must be soul-destroying for you and is quite mystifying to us."

Can you see why I find these people overpowering? They're allowed to be upset, but I'm not. If I am, it plays into the stereotype they have of me as someone who's negative and "holds on to every perceived slight." You know how it is in families: People have their assigned roles. In my family, I'm the screwy, remote little kid who flew the coop.

To be honest, there's a grain of truth in some of their criticisms of me and my husband. My husband can be antisocial. I can be moody and tend to remember negative things. But then, my brother (who's extremely funny and charismatic) can be thoughtless and dogmatic, and my sister (who's smart and capable) can be hyper-sensitive and condescending. I'm stunned they think that attacking us is the way to improve family harmony. It seems especially odd that they've known my husband for 21 years and are now saying that his behavior is unacceptable.

My brother and sister insist that they love me and have said these things because they want to "clear the air." I took the moral high road and have refrained from lashing out at them in return. Instead, I wrote them a calm letter, admitting some of their points but saying I disagreed with their methods. I figured, why hurt them the way they'd hurt me? But now I think I was wrong, and that I should have "cleared the air" right back at them, because I'm still seething.

My parents are getting older, and I don't want to sully their last years with petty quarrels. But maybe this one isn't so petty. I feel as though my siblings have crossed a line in the sand. Right now I'm not talking to either of them. Cary, you always have thoughtful and "different" advice, and I feel as though this situation could use some creativity. What do you think? Should I swallow my hurt for the sake of family harmony? Or will it fester and make things worse in the long run?

Estranged European

Dear Estranged European,

I THINK YOU did the right thing in not lashing out.

But beyond that, I have only my own sad experience, which mirrors your own. I can only share that with you, feeling as helpless as you do before these powerful and primal forces of the family. And what do I do with my own sad experience? I talk about it. I talk about it to my wife. I talk about it to my therapist. I write about it. I talk about it in recovery groups. I carry it around in a big, heavy bag across my shoulders. I carry it like a stone in my belly. Sometimes it goes up to my head and pounds my temples. Do I feel evolved? No. I feel like a fool. I can do nothing to improve it. It just sits there looking at me.

My older sister can pierce my heart with a harsh word and I'm a walking zombie for days. It is remarkable. And so we do not speak. Not lately. I just stay out of her yard.

It's very sad.

A radio interviewer asked me the other day does my own family ask me for advice? Wow. Ha ha ha. That was good.

But then I had to admit my younger brother did ask me for advice recently. My father, who is 84, spit out a molar at lunch. My brother asked me what to do? I told him not to try to glue it back in himself.

When you're a kid, you try to keep your siblings on your side. Were you like that? I was. I was in the middle: I had a lot of work to do—

keeping the thing together, mediating, working the art of the deal. It seemed like the older ones had our loyalty regardless, but I had to earn respect. I don't know why that is. But I was in terror of being out of favor. And I find it's still true. Like I say, one harsh word from my older sister and I'm a basket case.

If you move away for 20 years, then when you come back for these visits you have no ongoing business with your siblings about which you can negotiate. The practical reality of living together is a great thing; people figure out ways to make it work, to be civil. But you throw them together once every couple of years and they have neither the incentive born of necessity nor the skills born of practice to get along civilly and with good grace.

I've been reading Friedrich Engels' "The Origin of the Family, Private Property and the State" (it's on the book stack in the bathroom) and it has freed me a little from my hidebound and very narrow notions of family, broadening my view, as it were. And one other thing I have noticed is that with a spouse at least you have leverage; it would at least make some small difference if you left. The frightening thing about siblings you see only once a year is that you're leaving anyway. You don't have much to bargain with.

And think about family, or community, or tribe, in the broader, secular, non-blood way. When your biological family thousands of miles away is driving you insane, you need a functional family nearby. What family have you replaced your family with?

Maybe if you turn your attention to that question, and look for a feeling of belonging with people who really do seem to get you, who like you and respect you and will put up with you when you are feeling a little crazy, and who will feed you dinner ... that might help.

My sister is the
meanest person alive!

I don't want to shut her out of my life,
but her behavior is beyond the pale.

MY SISTER MAY be the meanest, most selfish person in the world. This sounds like a teenage taunt, but it's not.

When my mother was dying of cancer six years ago, my sister lived near my folks and never helped. She just walked into the house and complained about her husband, whom she divorced, messily and loudly, right as my mother was suffering the most.

She has an Ivy League master's degree, yet she gets fired constantly from jobs and hits my father up for money when she does. He bails her out, despite the fact that she isn't kind to him either. He recently has had a hip replaced, and she barely visited him or called him. I live out of state, and I flew in to help and I call all the time.

She walks into my father's house for family holidays and asks him what he has that she might sell for cash. At family events, she never cooks (despite being asked), can't wash any dishes due to what she calls a water allergy, and she talks incessantly about herself, never asking questions about others. Last year she gave us all Christmas presents with price tags still on them, telling me in particular that she'd "bought my earrings for herself, but didn't like them so she passed them on to me." Oh, and last Christmas, she had a meltdown in a restaurant, accusing me, my father, her boyfriend and my husband of being against her. It resulted in a family fight so bad that I haven't spoken to her since.

I think of myself as a pretty balanced person. I have a solid marriage, good friends, a nice relationship with my father and most of my in-laws. But this situation with my sister bedevils me—I just don't know how to relate to her! Even when we are in touch, it seems to be me calling her, her mooching meals or trips off me, and her complaining about how bad our childhoods were and how our parents were— fill in the blanks—control freaks, ADD, manic depressive ...

I remember a nice childhood with nice food, trips to Europe, good parents.

My question is, do I try to have a relationship with her at all, or do I cut my losses because she's incredibly toxic to be around? It feels terrible to say, but I feel like I'd like to divorce my own sister. Yet the thought of never having a decent relationship with her makes me sad.

Twisted Sister

Dear Twisted,

YOU CAN PROBABLY have some kind of tolerable relationship with your sister, though not necessarily the kind you'd consider ideal. The key is to understand her behavior well enough to set reasonable expectations.

If you knew, for instance, that she had a classic case of narcissistic personality disorder, then you could make some realistic predictions about her behavior.

So if I were you, I'd make an appointment with a psychologist who can consult with you about your sister's behavior. I would state that you want to get an understanding of your sister's personality so that you can better handle the upsetting family situations you are likely to encounter. A good psychologist could explain what various personality disorders are and how they affect family members, and also suggest kinds of behavior your sister is likely to engage in. That would help you prepare for whatever objectionable things she might do. It would also help you set limits on the kinds of interactions you're willing to have with her.

It is of course sad to contemplate never having a decent relationship with your own sister. But if you know what to expect, you can at least try to maintain some kind of relationship. Perhaps it would consist of regular, brief, highly structured interactions, held at a considerable distance. You might, for instance, decide to only send her greeting cards on holidays, and call her once or twice a year. That, at least, would be a relationship of sorts. It would shield you from the kind of painful episodes you have described, but it would maintain contact.

It's hard to set such limits with a family member, of course. One's expectations are often much higher; one really, really wants things to be a certain way; moreover one really believes, and justifiably so, that things ought to be a certain way in a family: Everyone ought to be loving and looking out for each other; everyone ought to show respect for the parents and try to give back some of what they've been given. It ought to be, you know, family-like!

While her self-centeredness does sound like a kind of narcissism, her breakdown in the restaurant sounds a note of paranoia. Now, wouldn't you think that the self-involvement and grandiosity of a narcissist would work against paranoia, making her feel invulnerable to plots against her? But perhaps a psychologist would say that these two conditions, paranoia and narcissism, work together at times, or alternate in a personality, one feeding the other. Or if one's narcissism is weak, for instance, then perhaps rather than being insulated by grandiosity against paranoia, one does indeed see oneself as the focus of the world but only in a weak, vulnerable, threatened way.

It's good to be realistic. But sometimes letting go of a hope for something better can be a letdown. To compensate for what you might feel as the loss of your sister, consider the many, many people with whom you can have better relationships. It might be most profitable to concentrate on them—your chosen family, as it were, rather than your given family. You can also work to strengthen the relationships you do have with other family members—your father, for instance, who may be victimized by his daughter in ways he scarcely understands or could admit to. He could maybe use some extra support, having also lost his wife only a few years ago. In this way, you can be a good sister and daughter, but also protect yourself.

Holiday home invasion

I don't want houseguests, I don't, I don't! But here comes my mom to complain about my air mattress!

Hello, Cary:

WELL, IT SEEMS to be that time of year again. I have spent the last 48 hours with a knot in my throat (and one in my shoulders, and a few in my back muscles), relishing that classic holiday feeling of having Disappointed the Family Once Again. I know it is an all-too-human experience, and that as such I should just roll with it ... but it seems so UNNECESSARY. There's got to be a better way.

Here's my ax to grind:

I am a single 37-year-old gal who has lived alone for the vast majority of my adult life (most recently, for the past 10 years). I enjoy living alone and realized sometime in my late 20s that I did not actually enjoy "entertaining at home" that much. While I still consider myself to be a warm, loving, sociable, fun person ... I do not choose to have people over to my house, and I do not choose to have overnight houseguests. I find that when forced to do so, I become edgy, uncomfortable with feeling 100 percent responsible for the guest's experience at every moment, and it rarely turns out to be a good time for me (or for my guests, I would imagine). I'm not saying this reaction is entirely neurosis free, but it is something I have recognized and (for now) accepted about myself.

My family, however, refuses to accept this and continues to insist on coming to visit. And I don't mean "coming to visit the town where I live"; I mean scheduling travel plans so that they will be sleeping at my house for a few days at a time. My discomfort with having company is no passive-aggressive thing that I keep hidden under a veneer of pretending that everything is fine, whilst standing in the kitchen obsessively sharpening the knives; I have said more times than I can count "I just don't really like having company. It's not anything against any of my loved ones, but I just end up uncomfortable." My family treats this like some subtle, vaguely insulting and not-funny joke.

So once again, I had company for the Thanksgiving holiday, and once again I ended up feeling like a failure because I wished that they had stayed elsewhere ... Like, perhaps, with the very close family friends (the ones with the four-bedroom house) who live about a mile from my place. My mother went home pissed off after spending four days sleeping on an uncomfortable air mattress and demanding a level of intimacy between us that I simply don't feel.

I love my mother very much, but (for a number of reasons) I tend to be a little bit more private than she would like. Instead of accepting this, she instead seems to ignore it for as long as she can ... and then gets her feelings hurt when we do not stay up all night with sleeping bags on the floor, telling secrets and giggling.

That's an exaggeration, Cary, but not by much. Some circumstances of my childhood resulted in a perhaps heightened urge toward self-protection in emotional relationships; I seem to have developed the hard-candy coating that may be typical to adults who went through abandonment and trauma as children. (My mom did the "I need to go find myself" thing and left me at age 5 with my sociopath father and an abusive, alcoholic stepmother. Mom came back and regained custody when I was 13, but I'm guessing that some of my less-than-ideal thought patterns were already well in place by then.)

I feel the need to repeat that I am a kind and loving person, and not some maladjusted shut-in. I truly love my family and genuinely enjoy their company—when it is meted out in such a way that I can now and then go home and spend alone-time with my dogs (instead of stressing about the guest towels in the bathroom). I just don't know what to say to my mom when she calls me a few days from now, acting bravely cheerful and yet still vaguely hurt. "I told you so" doesn't seem very gracious, now does it?

The Reluctant Black Sheep

Dear Reluctant Black Sheep,

IT'S REVEALING HOW you draw us in and then drop the bomb. Not liking to have houseguests sounds like an irritation and not much more, until we come to your mom abandoning you at age 5 to your sociopath father and abusive, alcoholic stepmother.

It is also, to my ear, both revealing and true to form how sophisticated and full of inner strength you sound; it's the familiar precocious self-reliance that neglected children acquire out of necessity.

I think this childhood abandonment was more a betrayal than you let on, and that it hasn't been dealt with the way it will need to be at some point; it's just been, as your words suggest, candy-coated. At the risk of torturing the conceit, there is below the candy coating some tender, tragic, melting sweetness that lives in fear of the day when the armor wears thin. It's not just sweetness either, if my guess is correct, but also a fiery rage always suppressed—because if it should ever burn with all its annihilating brightness, then your mom might really go for good, and you, as a 5-year-old, couldn't survive that, could you?

I'm not suggesting we pity you for what happened; I am suggesting you not minimize the enveloping nature of it, its centrality, its omnipresence. I suggest you begin instead like a scientist with a Geiger counter, searching out in every crevice the ancient echo of this abandonment, where like traces of the big bang it still crackles in the air.

Certain hypotheses are easy: For instance, to have your own home represents not just convenience, as your family seems to blandly assume, but survival. This one thing, in the face of abandonment, remains certain and true: Your four walls, your deadbolts, your own utility bills and kitchen paint, your own plants and cartons of milk in the fridge, your own direct line to the world unmediated by a mother on whom you know you cannot depend. How important these four walls are to you psychically! How powerfully any threat to them undermines your sense of well-being!

Now that Thanksgiving is over, you have survived another threat, only you are expected to pretend days later that it never happened, just as you were expected to pretend as a 5-year-old that you understand that your mother needs to go discover herself! As if the mother, wholly sufficient to the child, her very source of miraculous being, should be in some way insufficient to herself! How can that be? the 5-year-old might ask herself, unless the mother were fractured somehow? Or unless she, the 5-year-old, had injured her, or was insufficient to her happiness? How can it be that the source of my life, my blood, my food, my safety, should be insufficient to herself though wholly sufficient to me? And what does that mean about me? Am I not central to her existence, as she is central to mine? What have I done? Is it my failure to become fully competent in the area of potty training and speech that has caused her to become bored with me and seek more? How have I failed her that she's got to go off and discover herself? Who is this woman I thought was mine? And moreover who is this new woman with Daddy who stinks of medicine and can't walk straight, who stumbles and vomits and screams at me?

Sure, if the 5-year-old girl could think and speak, she might be saying things like that. But more likely only later would she formulate these thoughts verbally; they're just buried in her bones for now. They're buried in her ways, in her walls and floors, in her need to turn the lights out and hear not a sound, in her need to click the deadbolt and unplug the phone. I wish I knew the mechanisms in scientific terms, but I'm just guessing, the way the writers always have to guess, trying on shoes, throwing paint at the wall, inventing speech to answer our outrage.

This post-Thanksgiving blues sounds like the echo of an old abandonment and if I were you I would be so inconsolable and so angry I don't know how I would be able to mask it and forgive.

Does she not see that however dreamy her self-discovery seemed at the time it was the wrong thing to do? Have you ever discussed it with her? Has she ever broken down and said Yes, I see now that I was selfish and young, and yes, if I could, I'd redo it a different way, and you, my 5-year-old, would be the central shining joy of my young motherhood? Don't you long to hear that?

Meanwhile, maybe you can just get really tough. Don't ask. Insist. No family staying with you. None. Otherwise, your heedless mother, who perhaps has a little of the narcissist in her, will be walking through your walls for the rest of your life.

My family treats
my dad like dirt

*I can't believe the cruelty and I don't
know what to do.*

Dear Cary,

I HAVE BEEN living in New York City for the past 12 years. I origi-
nally come from a small, unimposing town in Massachusetts and, like
many people, I usually spend some part of the holidays visiting my
family. This year was no different. But I am finding that every time I
visit, however short and infrequent those visits may be, I just get more
and more enraged.

Here's a little background for you:

My dad is 70 years old and a recovering alcoholic. He hasn't had
a drink in approximately 25 years or so but, having never attended
12-step meetings, he still displays the "dry drunk" behavior that
comes with such a disease. He's never been a great provider, which has
caused my mother a great deal of frustration over the years. At heart,
however, he is a good man and an extremely loving father. He's also
the son of two alcoholics himself and came from an extremely fucked-
up family situation that no one could have gotten out of without some
amount of damage.

My mom, on the other hand, has always been the center of the family. She was the one who somehow managed to pay the bills on time
when my dad was bingeing, keep the children clean and well fed, and,
basically, keep things from falling apart. Obviously, this created much

anger and dissatisfaction for her over the years.

However, as tough as my mom has always been, there was another side to her. She was (and is) fiercely controlling. When it came to her home and her children, it was understood that she was in command. She was the disciplinarian and many of us lived in a certain amount of fear should we do something wrong—however slight.

Along with that control came a burning desire to always be right and always be needed. Her opinions were accepted as gospel. In addition, her children were taught from an early age that they could only get so far in life. College was out of the question (We don't have the money for that!) as was any kind of success whatsoever. We also had to suffer her angry mood swings. God help us if she came home from work in a bad mood. She would go from one of us to the other and rip us all to shreds with her words. In the end, all of her children were left with a troubled sense of self and very low self-esteem. I am the only one who moved away to achieve a modicum of success, although I have always been haunted by towering self-doubt.

As things are now, my mother and father are still living in the same house I was born in along with my oldest sister and only brother (both in their 40s). My siblings have no idea of the world outside of their little circle and are dangerously enmeshed with my mother who is, perhaps, even more controlling than she used to be. She has also managed to enlist my brother and sister against my father. This has resulted in my father becoming a literal shell of the man he once was. He is all of 100 pounds and spends most of his time being screamed at and verbally abused by my mother, my sister and my brother. His only respite is to smoke endless amounts of cigarettes out on the back porch, and drink coffee incessantly—actions that only seem to provide fuel for the fire. He eats little, is very unhealthy and, if I didn't know any better, I'd say he wants to die.

Whenever I return to Massachusetts (as I did for Christmas) I am enraged at their behavior. It is almost as if my mother has spent the last 25 years or so getting back at my dad for his drinking. She screeches at him, insults him and has made him her lackey. My brother, who is himself a mountain of anger, does nothing but bully him and my sister does the same. They believe my mother is an angel, possessed of nothing but generosity, kindness and selflessness. But they refuse to see the other side of her personality: that of a verbally abusive, controlling martyr/ monster. My dad has been stripped of every ounce of power, dignity and self-respect. And I don't know what to do.

Tired of Dad Bashing

Dear Tired,

I SEE YOU coming up the steps with your suitcase, the son who left, the son they fear, the son they find a little uppity now with his education and his job and his ideas, coming up the old steps you used to play on, carrying your suitcase into this haunted house, a little lost and blind in the sudden darkness after the winter sun, everything so incredibly dark and so incredibly the same after so many years, and you tug your suitcase a little tighter, your suitcase, your ticket to goodbye. And there's your father on the back porch smoking and drinking coffee, taking it and taking it and taking it because after all he was a drunkard all those years so it's his job to take it now, whatever they can dish out. After all he made them out of his own flesh and blood so whatever they've got, bring it on, he's got his coffee and his cigarettes, he's got his place on the back porch. He drank it all away so now he absorbs the blows, the insults, the daily onslaught of unrelieved resentment and fury and loss. There he is, killing himself, killing off his feelings with every puff, living on coffee and cigarettes till the end. And there you are carrying your suitcase through the house and finding him on the back porch and thinking, What in God's name am I going to do?

Maybe he'll say something like, "At least I'm keeping thin, son. Looks like you put on a little weight down there in New York City."

What in God's name can you do? Where do you even begin? And what do you say when your mom comes out and tells you not to bother with the old man, he's not worth it, and the old man chuckles like it's a fond old joke.

You could take him to a meeting, you know—those 12-step meetings he never went to enough of. You could call up and find out. Call AA, for heaven's sake, it's in just about every town on the planet, and ask if there's someplace for an old alcoholic to come and get some kindness and coffee—coffee no better than the stuff he's drinking now, and possibly worse, but free.

That's the only thing I can think of. He could go and spend some time with his kind—not his kin, who are eating him alive, but his kind, who will nod and say, Yeah, I know what you mean. Even once a week if he could just sit with other old guys who've blown it in perhaps far more spectacular ways than your dad—guys that have killed children on the highway in blackouts, guys that have awakened on desolate roads in unknown towns with inexplicable bruises, and guys that have just lived miserable little medicated lives of dim depression and unvoiced despair but who are now, amazingly enough, pretty much happy and OK!—if he could just spend some time with guys like himself maybe once a week, and maybe chuckle or just laugh out loud at it all, and let go, and learn how to live as an old alcoholic, maybe it might help.

But you're thinking, If only there was a way I could fix this awful family of mine—the way they treat him! Well, listen, my friend: Back slowly away from the hope. You're not fixing your family. Nobody is fixing anybody's family—not today, not any day.

The one guy you're concerned with is your dad. There are things you can do for your dad. I'd leave it at that. But that's plenty right there.

My mother=in=law, my mother=in=law, my mother=in=law!

I would like to see a very bad thing happen to my mother-in-law.

Dear Cary,

MY EIGHT-YEAR MARRIAGE has been to the perfect husband (12 years older), and has produced the perfect child. We are both emotionally and professionally fulfilled scientists. Our marriage is perfect, except for one thing—my mother-in-law. I want her to die. Violently. Now. And I want her to see it coming.

My husband had a childhood the Cleavers would envy. Born to uneducated parents, he and his sister were loved and had an idyllic, sunny existence. I, however, was horribly abused by highly educated parents, hit, kicked and told I was hideous, worthless and unlovable. I still love and forgive my parents, and keep in touch. Despite the terrible upbringing, I succeeded academically—as did my husband—and we found happiness in a safe, loving, mature relationship; we have never spanked or abused our child. Nevertheless, I wonder if my past colors the way I feel about my mother-in-law.

First, my mother-in-law initially irritated me with little things, like insisting that we invite 80 of her out-of-state friends (whom we didn't know) to our tiny wedding—we didn't. Then the irritations became rudeness. For example, once during a work commute, news of a school

66

shooting was broadcast on my radio. I phoned our home, where she was visiting, to ask her to turn on the TV and tell me what was going on. She knew my mom was a teacher in the school mentioned in the report, but she refused to go to the TV, saying that my father-in-law was watching something else. I had to wait until I got home an hour later to see the news myself. My mother was not shot, but people my family knew were killed.

Later, three days after my C-section, she and my father-in-law arrived, expecting a full Thanksgiving dinner to be hosted by me, tired and in pain. During this time, I got no sleep, could not bond with my child and had to be the maid, cook and entertainer.

Next, she visited uninvited on my first Mother's Day and took over, stealing my special day, insisting that attention be lavished on her. Often, when asked to pass my baby to me so that I could rock/feed/talk to her, she got upset or would simply ignore me. Many times she refused to hand my child to me at all. She persistently devalues me by asking me a question, getting an answer and then immediately asking my husband the same question in front of me. This is the routine even though he always gives her the same answer. She gets very upset when I disagree with her son, whom she worships. When I realistically portray his work (excellent but not flawless) she says I am jealous. She tells her friends he is getting the Nobel Peace Prize. (She means Nobel Prize for Science, but correcting her is hazardous.) She addresses our Christmas cards to Dr. and Mrs., although she knows I am a Ph.D., and she has been often corrected by my husband. She told everyone that we named our daughter after her, and when I told her that this wasn't true (it isn't), she became angry at me. Traditionally, when her feelings are hurt (by me, see instances above) she cries at mealtimes or gatherings, making everyone uncomfortable. And so on ... the petty list is long.

For the record, I am kind to her, honest and diplomatic, but when I speak the truth instead of pretending to be the sycophantic little woman who had no identity until I met her son, I am treated with derision and hostility. I am kind and fair to her even though it is difficult: She has a fourth-grade education, reads nothing, is witless and is terminally incurious about everything! I have never heard of a mother-in-law like this. She is not senile, and her family still insists that she is the most perfect little old lady. Also for the record, my usually perfect husband takes no stance and my father-in-law sides with her. How do I cope?

Invisible Daughter-in-Law

Dear Invisible Daughter-in-Law,

I WOULD VENTURE to say, amateur pretend psychologist that I am, that yes, your childhood very likely has something to do with your feelings toward your mother-in-law. I would also say that the thing about mothers-in-law is that you cannot get rid of them and you cannot change them. So in spite of the litany of behaviors you cite, your only recourse is to change yourself.

Not that there's anything wrong with you. Clearly, the one who has things wrong with her is the mother-in-law. Nonetheless, universal law of pop psychology: You're the one who has to change. Once you do this, you may end up feeling grateful to your mother-in-law as a catalyst, an agent of change. Bad events direct our attention to facts and we go, Hey, gotta do something now.

You say, "I want her to die. Violently. Now. And I want her to see it coming."

What those words say to me is this: You function in the professional world as a scientist, skilled in the old observe, hypothesize, test via experiment scenario. But in your emotional life you are not a scientist. You are, rather, a person trained in abuse. When you feel you are being abused, you react as you have been taught, as you learned in your household, by envisioning a scenario of harm.

Where physical violence is not going to solve anything, the scenario of vengeful harm is pointless. Even if you could harm her verbally in a subtle yet satisfying way, it would not solve your problem. Your problem is that you are hurt deeply—more deeply than necessary—by her thoughtlessness. You cannot change her thoughtlessness, so you must change how you respond to it. You know that throwing a hot pot of coffee at her or stabbing her with a kitchen knife is not going to help. But you are the product of an abusive household; those are the scenarios that arise in your mind.

You would still be trapped by your childhood, reacting to perceived slights with an outsize fantasy of violence and harm. You would still feel anxious and unsafe.

I'm also guessing, amateur psychologist that I am, that while you have gone to school and learned a whole new language with which to decode physical phenomena (do you work with the stars? with rocks? what kind of science do you do?), you have not been retrained emotionally. That is one of the best descriptions I have heard of psychotherapy—that it is emotional relearning.

It's not going to fix your mother-in-law. But the idea is to learn some techniques for dealing with emotional stimuli.

In the same way that science has axioms, the emotional life has axioms as well: Can't change other people. Have to change ourselves. Feelings aren't facts. Don't have to act on feelings. They are true, but not all that interesting or witty to repeat in conversation.

You can go through college for a liberal arts degree and fail to be educated about science. And you can go through college in science and fail to learn that you can't change other people.

So, anyway, I hypothesize: I think you can be helped by psychotherapy.

Please test this hypothesis experimentally and report the results.

My best friend has let me down for the last time

She always said she'd be there for me,
but when my son got sick, she wasn't.

Dear Cary,

MY GIRLFRIEND AND I grew up together and have always been like
sisters. She has always been a needy person: Nearly every day of my
life I've listened to her talk endlessly about her complicated relationships; I've held her hand as she freaked her way through countless
crises and meltdowns, and done a thousand favors for her. Through
all those years of offering hugs and help and sympathy and of taking
her side, I never asked much from her. Frankly, I didn't need it. She
always said that I was her best friend and she loved me, and if I ever
did need her, she'd be there for me. And I believed her.

Then, earlier this year, I almost lost my beautiful 10-year-old son to
a severe case of meningitis. The illness damaged his limbs, his kidneys
and his hearing, leaving him with permanent physical disabilities. My
husband and I needed all the support we could get to help our child
through this heartbreaking experience. Lots of people came through
for us, but my "best friend" was AWOL. I got the feeling she was begin-
ning to distance herself. We had a bunch of lame phone conversations
over the next weeks, during which she said that she knew I needed to
give all my attention to my family, so she was going to give me my space.
When I said I needed her help, she said that she was going through a
difficult time herself and was sorry that she couldn't be there for me.

Months later, it's as if we were strangers. Occasionally she'll call and leave brief messages like, "I'm thinking about you!" and "I miss you!" Recently, we invited some close friends and family over to celebrate our son's birthday. He's still healing from his illness, but we are so proud of how far he has come. I think everyone else got how special the day was for us. That morning, my friend called and bailed, with this story: She and her husband had argued the night before and she was "too depressed for a party." She wants to see us, she says, when things in her crazy, crazy life settle down.

That was the last straw. Something in me snapped. I get it now: She is an appallingly selfish bitch. She only "loved" me when I was available for her to use, and then she let me down. I hate her so much now that I am afraid the next time I see her, I might hurt her. I am so, so angry. Our families are close and we have friends in common, so I will have to see her during the coming holidays. I fantasize about slapping her in front of everyone. I have dreams in which I beat her and draw her blood. How can I let go of this terrible anger and move on?

Reformed Sucker

Dear Reformed Sucker,

YOU'RE NOT A sucker. You just took her at her word and thought she would come through but she didn't and instead she broke your heart. You don't have to be a sucker for that to happen.

If there were a short answer to your question it would be that you can let go of this terrible anger by moving through it to what comes next, a shaking of the head and a bitter shrug, a sad perplexity, the uncomprehending Why? of the unaccountably injured, or perhaps what we call acceptance. But that would only be part of it.

People say there are definite stages to it, but I don't know. They say there are five stages of grief or whatever. They say it as if everybody knows. I don't know. I never memorized that. I think you make up your own stages. Whatever stage you need to be in, however your house is arranged, whatever you've got room for, that's where you go when you're done with the anger. The only thing certain is that you move from anger into something that is not anger. Anger is heat and it always cools. Anger always cools just like the evening always comes.

So why should I tell you something pompous and all-knowing like you will move from this stage to that stage? And why should I speculate about what calamities she has undergone, calamities that though tiny loomed so large in her life that she had this appalling failure of heart?

It might be a sign that you're gaining some distance if you find yourself one day, maybe a year or two from now or maybe 10 years from now, wondering in a not particularly emotional way just what little torments were consuming her that made her so useless to others. Did she have a pile of traumas to inventory? Was her husband burning her with cigarettes? But it would be a long time from now that you would be thinking about that. For now there is simply your anger at the bitter loss of your friend.

Aw, shit. People fail you, they do, they let you down when you need them, they get suddenly dense when you need them to be smart, they fold when you need them to open up, they close right before you get there and sleep through your honking horn in the snow. "I know she's in there, where else could she be? Why doesn't she come to the door?" People fail you, they do, they let you down when you need them. They don't say they're sorry because they don't even know. That's how dense they are. (And maybe wounded, too, in ways we can't see, but we're not in a mood for sympathy, are we?)

I say this speaking to you as a friend who himself has let people down from time to time but who will goddamn it be there in a pinch when it is really necessary, always always always, even if I am going through something. I will be there.

But that is so easy to say! "I will be there." That's what she said, isn't it? But she never had a clue how to do it! Yes, she was always promising to come through one day and then the day comes and you tell her in plain English, "This is your day! Your payment is due! It's time for you to be there for your friend!" and she can't hear it.

And then, when for one nanosecond it did indeed dawn on her that you really did need help she offered you ... space! Who in her right mind who knows anything about helping thinks that giving you space is helping? Giving you space is just being absent.

Are you planning to strangle her, really? Have you got a rope? You're not, are you? But you're afraid of how much you want to hurt her. So what are you going to do when you walk into the warm cocktail music evening and she comes tripping down the carpet loaded with a hug? It's going to make you angry, isn't it, when she aims that hug at you and starts to pull the trigger?

So maybe you'd better meet with her before any of these random occasions occurs. Maybe you'd better track her down and confront her so you get to say your piece the right way, in your own time. I know she should come to you and help you, for God's sake, but you're the one who has to do it. You're always the one who has to do it. I know that. This time, however, you are not tracking her down merely so she can fail you all over again. You are tracking her down so you can tell her once and for all what you need to tell her.

Tell her and do not apologize and do not forgive her and do not think about the future in which all is forgiven. It may be that all is forgiven in the future. All is not forgiven right now. Right now you just have to tell her.

I'll be alone for Christmas—merrily!

Do not pity me: I prefer solitude.

Dear Cary,

HERE'S A TIMELY topic for you. Please address this not just for me, but for thousands of others who are alone for the holidays.

I'm divorced and childless, I broke up with my boyfriend last month, my friends are busy with their families (most of them out of town), my father and two brothers died over 10 years ago, and my mother is a thousand miles away living with her third husband near his large family. Therefore, I have no plans for Christmas.

I'm not Scrooge. I put up lights. I sent out cards. I baked cookies and bought gifts for people I care about, and I shipped them. I'm planning to buy something nice for myself, too. I have presents to open, and every day brings cards from distant friends. I'm not a recluse—I work two jobs, one full time and one part time, so I'm around people almost every day. I have a couple of parties to go to, and I expect to have a good time. But on Christmas Day, it will be just me and the cats, curled up on the couch, drinking champagne, watching a good movie or two. And that's fine!

I am OK with being alone. It's not the first time, and I was OK then too. I'm an atheist, so there is no religious significance to the holiday for me. I enjoy my own company; I live alone. Being alone is not the problem.

The problem is that my mother will not stop pitying me for being alone, no matter how many times I tell her it doesn't bother me. It's as though she wants me to be miserable, so she keeps asking if I don't have someone to be with. As if being with just anyone would have to be better than what I have planned. Then again, she is the one who stays married to a man she doesn't like very much just because she's afraid of being alone.

I know from experience that being with just anyone solely because it's Christmas is a recipe for disaster. I've tried spending Christmas with Mom and her husband's large family—now there's an experiment in terror. I was "Harry's wife's child by a former marriage," unknown, unnamed and deeply pitied for being "not one of us (poor thing)." Never again.

I spent Thanksgiving alone this year too. It was fun. I cooked a turkey feast for myself, ate dinner on the good china and shared my leftovers with those less fortunate. I gave thanks for the fact that I wasn't forced by tradition to spend the day with anyone I didn't like. I didn't spend a nanosecond feeling depressed or lonely.

Please, Cary, say something about spending Christmas alone that isn't depressing. All you ever hear or read is "spending Christmas alone is hard."

I say it isn't, and there's no reason to wallow in self-pity just because society (and your mother) keeps telling you there's something wrong with being alone and content.

Solitaire

Dear Solitaire,

WHY SHOULD YOUR choice to be alone on Christmas bother people?

Let's be fair. Some are probably genuinely concerned. You are alone in part because of the deaths of your brothers and your father, your divorce, your childless status and a recent breakup. Those conditions evince concern in those who love you. When they think of you alone on Christmas they think of these things.

But they do not speak of these things directly, do they? I'm guessing that, out of delicacy of feeling or a lack of words, they speak around these things. They say, Oh, you really can't be alone on Christmas, how sad! And you think, what an interfering dolt this loving relative is; what an intrusive ninny is this person who is supposed to be my friend!

Ideally, you and they could be frank; you could share your feelings and thoughts in an atmosphere of mutual respect. You might admit that of course these things happened and had they not happened you might not be alone, while also making clear that, given the alternatives, being alone suits you quite well. And perhaps you can indeed have such frank conversations with your friends. But not with your mother or her new family.

So you do not have a chance to make yourself understood. Instead, whatever true concern there may be emerges distorted, as controlling and manipulative behavior.

Argh!

Too bad we can't all be more frank with each other and say, OK, suit yourself.

There is also the matter, this time of year, of mass behavior. Everyone is expected to participate. Annoying as this may be for cultures that do not include Christmas as part of their traditions, it is also annoying for those of us raised in the culture but wishing to have some control over how we pass through these days. Every year, it feels like all the secular autonomy we have so desperately struggled for over the years passes out of our hands when we are dealt the annual trump card of Christmas. Sure, play your hand the rest of the year as you see fit. Pretend to be independent the rest of the year. That's all very cute. But this is Christmas, damn it! Resume your family role!

I celebrate your independence as I celebrate the independence of this nation from all superstitious tyranny.

The crowd is a tyrant, and you must resist. By resisting the tyranny of Christmas, you save your own soul.

So even as I sing carols and pop popcorn, I will think of you on Christmas day with envy.

And a Letter from Cary

Cary's crappiest Christmas ever

My last Christmas was the worst one yet—
and I have the scars to prove it!

TODAY IS SUNDAY, Oct. 17, 2010, exactly 10 months since I went into surgery on Dec. 17, 2009.

I plan to have a better Christmas this year than I did last year.

That should not be difficult.

But before I get into all that, let me say what's coming and why. It wasn't until we had these columns selected and put together that I realized I ought to say something about how I get through the holidays, and why I feel a special bond with people for whom the holidays are difficult. They are difficult for me. I know some of the reasons why. But as I thought of it, I realized, as if for the first time—because this is how one processes enormously difficult experiences—that my 2009 Christmas was the weirdest, most uncomfortable Christmas ever. I guess it was so weird that I forgot it was Christmas.

Now some of this is kind of gross, and you should know that. I haven't really gone into all the effects of my cancer surgery until now. I'm planning to write a memoir about it and hope this doesn't screw up the deal with the publishers by talking about it first here. I think it's a good idea to talk about this stuff so that other people in the same situation may take some courage from my story.

This has been written quickly, without my usual agonizing (!) attention to detail (ha ha) so please cut me some slack. I'm just trying to let you know what happened. (And look at it this way: You're getting a story nobody else is getting.)

So anyway, last Christmas night I was standing in my bathroom at home, a week out of major surgery, covered with my own shit, trying to figure out what had happened to me, and how I was going to clean myself up when I couldn't bend from the waist or sit, and had these two rubber tubes coming out of my back and stitches covered with dressings on my belly and all across and up and down my butt. The stitches were very delicate and had to be kept clean and dry. I could not bend or they might come apart. I'd been opened up and taken apart and had to be put back together.

I was high on painkillers and not thinking too clearly or I would have screamed to my wife downstairs to wake up and come help me. But instead, I thought I had things pretty well under control. She needs her sleep, I thought. I should let her sleep and figure this out on my own.

I was thinking, Where had this shit come from? I mean, obviously it came out my ass. But I mean, how had this happened? I had stepped in it. I was on my way to the bathroom and I felt this gooey stuff on my toes, and this lump in my pajamas, and I was kind of mystified. What is this?

Oh, shit, I know what this is. This is shit. This is my own shit. Oh, shit.

That was last Christmas.

Today, I am feeling great. I have just had a really good swim. In my slow recovery from cancer surgery, I have been swimming since mid-June, when I first jumped into the pool at the Dynasty Suites motel in Redlands, California, where I was staying while getting proton beam radiation therapy at Loma Linda Hospital. That first plunge was a gingerly swim. Since then I have been swimming moderately, slowly increasing in intensity.

Today, I sprinted in the water for the first time. I sprinted a lap in the fast lane, rested, sprinted again. I sprinted a few times. It felt great. Wow. I am coming back physically. I was blowing away the other swimmers. Of course, I could only last a lap or two sprinting. But it felt good to go fast, to exert, to exhaust myself. So now that I am exhausted, I figure, yep, I should go home and write a new intro to the collection of holiday columns. Oh, yeah. What better way to give a good, positive message than to tell how I spent last Christmas?

So here is the good Christmas/bad Christmas continuum. For a while we had the total good Christmas thing figured out. We would go to Manka's. Manka's was this restaurant in Inverness, California, where we ate on our wedding night. We didn't know about it beforehand but after our wedding—this was in September 1993—we drove up the coast to the Tomales Country Inn and the innkeeper there, Laura Hoffman, told us if we wanted a good meal we should drive down to Inverness and go to Manka's. So we did. And Norma had this notion that since she was only going to wear the wedding gown this one day, she ought to get as much out of it as possible, so she kept her wedding gown on for dinner. That was pretty cool. People were definitely looking at us. People were taking pictures. and it was one of the best meals ever. Manka's was legendary. Alice Waters dined there with Prince Charles. It was that kind of a place. Then it burned down. On Dec. 26, 2006, it burned down while we were in Austin, Texas celebrating Christmas with Norma's mom. We were going to eat there that year but, well, we went to Texas.

So we've had good Christmases and we've had fucked up ones and I always get upset and wiggy around Christmas because my expectations are high. I always expect music and joy and peace on earth and all that.

But having had this Christmas last year where I was standing in the bathroom covered with shit, unable to bend, full of painkillers, beset with shooting pains down my left leg, half my midsection still numb, and having to use a straight catheter to pee, well, I'm kind of happy now that I'm just alive and not in pain and living indoors. And I hope you can be too.

Some Christmases are just better than others.

The surgery on Dec. 17, 2009, was long, complex and demanding. There was a colorectal surgeon, a neurosurgeon and a plastic surgeon. The whole thing was slated to take about 14 hours. First they made a big incision from my navel down to my pubis and the colorectal surgeon went in and moved my bowel and intestines out of the way. She had to do that from the front. That alone was a big deal. And they didn't know what they might find in there. They thought if the tumor had gotten into the intestine, then they were going to have to cut a hole in my belly and give me a colostomy. I was all prepared for that. They had marked me with a special pen and everything. I'd gone to a specialist who made me walk around and show her how I wore my pants so if they put the colostomy in my belt wouldn't rub against it. As it turned out, the colorectal situation was OK, they didn't need to give me a colostomy, so they just shoved my junk over far enough so then they could turn me over and the neurosurgeon and the plastic surgeon could get to work sawing off the end of my sacrum and cutting out the tumor with wide margins around it. So they turned me over and they cut this enormous incision in my back, down there by the tailbone, and then these other lateral incisions across my butt, like in the shape of a big smile across my butt.

It's really weird in the showers at the gym. I don't think anybody else has an incision quite like this. Because what I had was really rare and the doctors, well, they were really remarkable people. It was a sacral chordoma. Did I mention that? So what they had to do there was take out the tumor but also basically cut off the lower part of my sacrum. And the thing is, your gluteus maximus, or butt muscle, well, it originates at your ilium, your sacrum and your coccyx, and they were going to cut off the coccyx and the lower part of the sacrum, so the two halves of that muscle would have nothing to connect to there, so the plastic reconstructive surgeon had to connect the left butt muscle to the right butt muscle, if you can imagine that. So after they took out the tumor and the messed-up bone, that's what they did. The sacrum was all fucked up from the tumor chewing away at it and eating into it. So they did all that on Dec. 17, 2009.

The plan was that I would be in the hospital for two to four weeks and then I would be in a rehab place for six weeks while I learned to walk again. I would not be able to sit for a minimum of six weeks. I could lie down, and I could stand. But I could not sit. I could not bend that way. That might tear the butt muscles that had been stitched together.

Plus, right after the surgery and for a good time afterwards, I could not lie on my back or on my stomach. The only way I could sleep was on my side. And I had to be turned. And they had these two drainage tubes in my back that were kind of painful to roll over and delicate.

So everything went great. The surgery went great. In the intensive care unit after surgery, the plastic surgeon came in and had them take the dressings off my butt so he could see his work and he stepped back and said, "Mr. Tennis, I like what I see."

Like I say, it's now Oct. 17, 2010, and guess what else? It's the first day of rain. I wait every year for the first rain. The first rain streaks down the window pane and I'm glad. The long, rainless summer is over. And I'm strong. I've been swimming. I sprinted. But this is about Christmas. We're getting there. The San Francisco Giants are going to play the Philadelphia Phillies this evening in the second game of the National League pennant race. Artur Rubinstein's Chopin mazurkas are on the stereo. I'm sitting in the gray light of the first rain of 2010. I smell of the pool. I'm drinking the anti-cancer gen mai cha green tea. I'm healthy.

You know what else? It's the 21st anniversary of the Oct. 17, 1989, Loma Prieta earthquake. Not sure what that means. I'm just saying.

But back to the hospital. So my first few days of recovery I was on great pain drugs but still the pain was pretty awesome. But here is how I came have my strangest Christmas ever.

In the hospital I had what they call a great attitude. I think I had decided to have a great attitude because what else can you do? I wanted this to be a good experience. Some people talk about cancer and wanting to beat it. I wasn't really like that. I wasn't thinking about beating it. I don't really know how to beat it. I don't even know what it is or what beats it. What I wanted to do was just maintain high spirits. I suppose you might say I did not want to be defeated by it, and that might be the same thing as wanting to beat it, but mainly I was focused on me. I wanted myself to be upbeat and in high spirits. I like to be that way. And the drugs helped. Does that distinction make sense? I guess what I'm saying is that I wasn't focused on the cancer. I was focused on how I wanted to feel and behave.

I also like to show off. I like to excel. I like to do well. So about five or six days into my stay in the hospital a social worker came along, I think she was a social worker, and said she wanted to see if I could get out of bed and walk. I was gung ho. I was, Let's do this. I was, Show me the way out of here. It was something to do.

Getting out of bed was tricky. You had these two tubes coming out of my back, and you had these intravenous fluids and all this crap, and you had my very delicate stitches going all up my belly and then back there up my lower spine and across my butt, that big smile of stitches back there, and the stitches were all still in there, and it was pretty delicate, and the two drainage tubes coming out of my back, so it was a big operation getting me vertical but I was all for it. So there I was vertical. And there I was walking. Wow. That was exciting. I was like, Let's go. Let's go walking. They were all steadying me and cautioning me but I was like, Let's go here, let's go walking around the hospital. I shuffled Frankenstein-like down the hall. Then we came to this thing, a set of steps that led nowhere. Like a useless bunch of steps. She says, Can you go up the steps? And again, loving a challenge, I kind of bounded as best I could. Well, I didn't bound. But I gingerly went up the steps. I went up all of them and then I came down again. So that was amazing. They were all impressed. I was proud of myself. I was like a little kid showing off. It was like we were having a party.

But it was a trick. That's what I didn't realize. It was a trick to get me out of the hospital.

There was no way I wanted to leave the hospital. I was in no condition. You'd have to be crazy. Me go home? You have to be kidding.

I was showing off how I could walk but that didn't mean I was ready to go home.

So I guess this was like Dec. 23rd when I went for my big walk, showing off to the social worker and the nurses, gliding down the hall, waving to the other patients. Me going up the stairs, showing off my good balance and my athletic abilities, making the turn, showing off my spin move. "Want to see my spin move?" I asked. I was joking around. This was fun.

But it was a trick to get me out of the hospital. I was an idiot. I should have hammed up the lameness. I should have moaned and groaned and claimed I couldn't move a single step.

Then came this business about wouldn't I love to be home for Christmas? Not really. I wasn't really into going home for Christmas. But here were these nurses, this one nurse in particular, this bouncy, competent, impressive and pretty blond nurse saying wouldn't I love to be home for Christmas? Wouldn't that be great? And me wanting to make these poor suckers feel like I'm not taking their efforts for granted, like I appreciate them. I'm like, Yeah, sure, that would be great. But I'm thinking, No way. No way this suffering hulk of wounded flesh is going home for Christmas. What about my intravenous pain meds?

So then Christmas Day comes and they're all like, Well, you're going home. And I'm like no way, call my doctor. But there was this business about no way your insurance is going to pay for you to stay in the hospital if you can walk and go up and down stairs.

And you don't want to stay in the hospital anyway, do you? What with all the diseases going around the hospital, and the risk of infection? And I'm like, Yeah, I damn well do want to stay in the hospital.

So there was this thing about peeing and pooping and passing gas. After a big surgery like that, your innards shut down, as I understand it. For a few days there, I couldn't have any solid food. I was just having liquid stuff intravenously and some coffee I think. And then one day I had solid food. That was kind of ridiculous but it was solid food. We made a video. And then they were coming around on the fifth and sixth day asking if I'd passed gas. I don't think I'd passed gas.

What I did not understand fully, and I can't blame them for not explaining this in detail, although I wish they had, is that I had lost my third, fourth and fifth sacral nerves, the ones that control bowel, bladder and sexual function. That was it in a nutshell. But I didn't really get that right then. I didn't really know what was up with me and digestion and all that.

To tell the truth, it was pretty great to just be in bed, on heavy pain meds, with one of those buttons on a cord that you reach up and press and get Dilaudid whenever you need it. That was pretty great. I was high. I was really high and enjoying it. But all those drugs, of course, stop the digestive system. I'd hardly eaten anyway. Except I sneaked a banana. That was against the rules but I did. So where were we?

Oh, yeah, so the nurses keep asking if I've passed gas. And I'm like, I don't think so. And then they have me get up and walk to the bathroom to see if I can pee. And I can't really pee. I can't pee and I am not passing gas and I don't know what this all means but they're all like, Won't you be excited to go home for Christmas?

Merry Christmas.

What?

You want to get me an ambulance?

No ambulance.

No ambulance? What kind of place is this? No ambulance? I can't sit down. How am I going to ride in a car home?

You could get a van.

What?

At that point it was pretty weird. They were telling me there was no ambulance to take me home, but I was going home, and I couldn't sit in a car seat, and still this business about have you passed gas and can you pee?

Of course I can't pee.

So what they did was put me on a gurney and then we got all these pillows and piled them up in the car and put the front seat down and somehow got me off the gurney and into the car and I lay on my side and we did the trip home. And I'm being a hero the whole way.

And that was my Christmas. We came home and I ate all this food that people had made. Our friends had made all this food. And I ate all this great food at home and we made me a bed on the couch and I lay down and watched TV and took a bunch of pain meds and you gotta understand ...

Oh, yeah, but before, since I hadn't peed yet, and since the whole time in the hospital I'd had a Foley catheter in, so when I was getting ready to go home, this pretty nurse had come in and showed me how to use a straight catheter. Now this is a rubber tube you stick up your dick. You clean off the head of your penis first with this povidone iodine on a cotton swab, and you sterilize your hands with Purel, then you grease up the thin rubber tube with KY jelly, and then you put a little KY jelly on the tip of your dick, and then you stick the tube up your dick. Yourself. And then when the tip of the catheter finally gets inside your bladder, pee comes out the end of the catheter and you drip it into one of those plastic urinals with markings on it for how much you peed.

So this whole catheter thing seemed like kind of an afterthought, after everybody's decided I'm going home. So this pretty nurse comes and shows me how to do this thing with the straight catheter. And then she says, OK, you do it. So I did it and it was kind of like not a big deal, except it was way strange to be doing it. But I'm still not getting in my head the full extent of how my life has changed. I'm not getting that those nerves are gone.

So we get me home, and we have this kind of Christmas party, with some friends in the house, and we eat all this food, and it's really great to be home and have all my friends here and be eating all this food, but then we're both pretty exhausted so Norma goes to bed and I stay up on the couch. It seemed like the logical place, because I was not going to be sleeping much and I would be waking her up and I was so delicate with these tubes coming out of me I didn't think I should be sleeping in a bed with anybody else in it. It just seemed logical that I should stay on the couch.

So I lie down for a while and then around midnight I get up and start walking, and I step in this shit. I'm like, what is this shit that I have stepped in? Then I realize it's my own shit. I have shat my pajamas. And then I go in the bathroom and, now, realize, I can't bend. I can't bend at all. I have tubes coming out of me. I have stitches in my butt and in my abdomen. And I have shit all over me. I have stepped in it and I have it on my leg and on my foot and it's just coming out of me. Nobody really explained this situation. Nobody said, Dude, you've got to start wearing Depends now, because you've got no anal sphincter muscle, those nerves are gone and we don't know what all is going to happen eventually, you may get it back, but for right now, here, you'd better wear these diapers.

Nobody told me that.

Now, I'm kind of an idiot. It's true. I am. And sure, in this situation in the bathroom with the shit all over me, I would like some help. But I am not sure I really want my wife in on this. I mean, she can—and did—deal with some pretty raw, fucked-up stuff, in amazing manner, with a calm and loving determination that I will never forget. But in my drugged-up state, standing there in the bathroom, I did not want to be yelling for her to wake up and come up there and help me.

I wanted to handle this on my own. I wanted to be ingenious. But I had these tubes coming out of me, and these stitches, and this dressing over the stitches, so I couldn't just get in the shower and wash all this off. That was what I wanted to do. I just wanted to wash that shit off. I wanted to get in a hot shower and just get clean. But I couldn't do that, because of the dressings and the stitches. And I couldn't sit down, and I couldn't bend. So I stood there in the bathroom covered with shit trying to figure out what to do.

Merry Christmas. Somehow I got out of my pajamas. I got into the tub. I stood in the tub with a washcloth.

I cleaned myself up. That's pretty much it. But would you like to know what happened the next morning?

The next morning, which would be Boxing Day, I wake up and things are not so great. I'm not feeling so terribly great. In fact, I feel awful. I have a pain in my belly, right behind my navel. I'm sweating and feverish. I feel nauseous. I tell my wife, I think I need to go back to the hospital. This is not good at all. I think you'd better call the hospital.

So she calls the hospital and tells them I've got this pain behind my navel and I'm feverish and sweating and nauseous and the first thing the nurse says is, has he catheterized himself? And I'm like, no. I, uh, forgot.

You know, you don't think about peeing all that much, ordinarily, do you? I mean, you pee when you have to pee. You don't schedule peeing. You don't, like, every four hours get out your peeing apparatus and grease it up and get your container and measure how much pee you make. I mean, you don't, do you, unless you have a medical situation?

I had a medical situation but had not really thought about having a medical situation. It hadn't sunk in. I hadn't really thought about the fact that what this meant was I had to do this peeing thing all the time. Weird, huh? How you don't really think these things through. You go along as though life were the way it used to be.

So the nurse on the phone says, real urgent and serious now, he has to use that catheter *right now.* So my wife comes and says, You have to do that catheter thing *right now.* I can see she's upset. She's angry. And I'm angry. I'm also chagrined and stupefied. So here is the thing about that. I can't sit up. I have to lie on my side on the couch, with those tubes coming out of my back, and somehow do the thing with swabbing the head of my penis with the povidone iodine swab, and then put the KY jelly on it, and on the thin rubber catheter, and then slide it up inside my dick but meanwhile I've got to hold this urinal bottle and keep the end of the thing inside there so when the urine starts coming out it'll go in there. Or did we even have one of those then? Or did we use like some other kind of bottle? Did we use a liter Gerolsteiner mineral water bottle? I think we did. I remember fearing that when it got to the top it was going to overflow and I wouldn't be able to stop the pee coming out of the tube because I've got no bladder sphincter or urethral sphincter muscle anymore. I mean, the muscle is there but the nerve that connects to it is gone. So I can't will myself to pee and I can't stop myself from peeing. It's out of my hands. So I just watch the bottle fill up with pee and pray that it stops.

It stopped.

But I could have died.

I could have died and they didn't really explain this to me, and they didn't send home a nurse with us, and they didn't arrange for home nursing care or a home health aide. We were shell-shocked and alone, and it was Christmas, and the day after Christmas.

So basically last Christmas sucked. So this Christmas is going to be better. I guarantee it.

Like, what could go wrong?

So the deal is, things can get really bad, and then you can get through it, and then you can decide, OK, that was bad enough, so I'm going to make sure that next Christmas is good.

I recommend you do that. Find what you can enjoy in the holidays and let the rest go. It gets better.

And I feel like that's not a great ending. Like it's not all deep and beautiful like some of my stuff. But it'll have to do.

Like I say, it gets better.

Cary Tennis
Sunday, Oct. 17, 2010
San Francisco